It's a wonderful new life!

The Don Double Story

EILEEN F. M. THOMSON

KINGSWAY PUBLICATIONS
EASTBOURNE

ISBN 0 86065 141 X

Unless otherwise indicated, Scripture quotations
are from the Authorized Version (crown copyright).

Printed in Great Britain for
KINGSWAY PUBLICATIONS LTD
Lottbridge Drove, Eastbourne, E. Sussex BN23 6NT by
Richard Clay (The Chaucer Press) Ltd, Bungay, Suffolk.
Typesetting by Nuprint Services Ltd, Harpenden, Herts.

Contents

Preface

The renewal of the Holy Spirit in the church in recent years has brought us into an era where miracles, healings, visions and prophecy have become, if not exactly commonplace, not nearly as rare as they used to be.

The Don Double story makes exciting reading—supernatural happenings and thrilling answers to prayer abound. All are bonafide accounts, many of which can be confirmed by numerous witnesses.

The story is not written to exalt a man—particularly one who has not yet even finished his course. Rather it is written as a testimony to the grace and power of God.

'I imagine it would be difficult to capture Don in print,' commented one Anglican minister, 'because, well, he's larger than life.' That is a good description of the 46-year-old evangelist, physically and spiritually.

Because of the anointing which rests upon him, there is a tendency among some to regard Don with awe. But to those who have the advantage of knowing him more intimately, he is recognized simply as a good man who walks humbly with God. 'Don doesn't see himself as anyone special,' friends testify, 'he's completely open to the Lord. That's why God can use him.'

I can count it a privilege to have been asked to write this story and I pray that the same anointing will be upon it as rests upon all the Good News Crusade ministry.

EILEEN F. M. THOMSON

1

Posting and Posters

Regimental policeman Don Double, of the Royal Army Medical Corps in Aldershot, turned uneasily in his bunk. Someone was shaking him roughly by the shoulder. Wasn't it bad enough having to get to sleep in broad daylight without some fool waking you up again?

'Go 'way,' he muttered irritably, 'Go a. . . .'

'Double!' The voice penetrated his slumbers with the clarity of a fire alarm. He shot up in bed. A large staff-sergeant stood glaring at him—stick in hand.

'Double, did you have a motor-cycle out last night?'

'I, er . . . yes sir, yes I did,' he mumbled in confusion, rubbing his eyes.

'Right! Then you're in for it Double!' the sergeant replied grimly, as Don jumped to attention.

Wide awake now, memory surged back. Don felt a wave of dismay and resentment sweep over him.

Night patrol every three weeks could be pretty boring! He and his pal had only borrowed someone's motor-cycle from the back of the NAAFI to do their rounds. His partner had driven it while he sat on the back. It made a bit of a change. Quite a lark in fact.

Of course they had replaced the bike, but didn't know that one of the NAAFI girls hearing them come in had looked out of the window. 'It was the big tall policeman,' she reported. A sure identification.

Just like that old mean-man of a sergeant to question

him while he was still half asleep, Don fretted. If only he'd had his wits about him he would have answered, 'No,' or concocted a suitable story to cover himself.

Too late now! The inevitable followed. Don and his friend were charged, demoted, given fourteen days confinement to barracks, and then posted.

Having reduced the two men to the status of private, the army now deemed it necessary to send them away from Crookham Base for their own good. Some of the rank and file might otherwise try to get their own back on the erstwhile policemen, who had formerly been responsible for their security and discipline.

Fourteen days of miserable confinement to barracks passed slowly. Then the postings. Don hurried anxiously to the Company Orders Notice Board. 'Private Double to Catterick Camp,' he read.

'Oh no! Not Catterick,' Don groaned. Catterick had a terrible name among the men—a most unpleasant, even notorious camp. What rotten luck! Then a novel idea occurred to him. 'I'll pray about it,' he decided.

Don at this stage knew nothing about real prayer, his church contacts having been merely formal ones.

His own description of himself at that time is graphic, 'Drunkard! Liar! Thief! King of Dirty Jokes!' Strange he should decide to pray.

'God,' he began naively as he lay in bed that night, 'God, I don't want to go to Catterick. I'm asking you to send me to Colchester,' the latter being only twelve miles from his mother's back door.

After the prayer a strange feeling of optimism and confidence took hold of Don. Although he knew nothing about the principles of faith, he started to tell his pals in the depot, 'I'm going to Colchester.'

'You're crazy, Double. It's up on Company Orders that you are to go to Catterick.' 'Fourteen days C.B. has turned Double's head.' 'He's got a screw loose,' they jeered. But the young soldier remained stubbornly convinced.

Twenty-four hours before Don was due to leave camp, bags packed in readiness, a new order appeared on the notice board which read, 'Private Double's posting has been changed. He will leave on the 8 a.m. train tomorrow for Colchester.'

Convinced as Don had appeared to be, when it really happened he reeled with amazement and shock. So God did answer prayer! God was 'for real'. Moreover, it seemed that He would even take an interest in a godless and mischievous young man.

Why! God had more power than all the generals, colonels, and majors of the British Army put together. What a shattering discovery. Next day, shaken but exultant, Don took his departure from Aldershot.

Following his arrival in Colchester, Private Double began to serve as a male nurse in the military hospital, even learning to give injections. He enjoyed the work, especially appreciating the opportunity afforded to get home to Hadleigh for long weekends quite frequently.

Outwardly then, circumstances could be said to be quite congenial. Yet inwardly Don experienced turmoil. Disturbed by the revelation of the reality of God, fear and a sense of guilt hung over him. In addition, an unnerving experience while serving on the officers' ward did nothing to help his state of mind.

The ward sister sent Don to check up on a newly arrived patient who had been a fantastically long time in the bathroom. Don knocked—no answer. He called—no response. He then climbed over the bathroom partition to find the unfortunate man hanging by his dressing gown cord—a suicide!

Shortly after this tragic incident, Don was sent to a little Medical Reception Station known as Westoffs, near Thetford, where he spent the last three months of his national service.

His next free weekend found him rummaging around his old room at home, looking for his Bible of Sunday School days. Dusting it off, he carried it back to Thetford, and set about the mammoth task of trying to read it.

He hadn't a clue where to begin, so started at the back—at Revelation! Having little education, Don found reading of any kind difficult.

Not surprisingly his Bible reading produced no great success. He understood next to nothing. Even had he done so, the subject matter of the Apocalypse was hardly such as would have subdued his fears, and the fact that his room lay next to the mortuary only aggravated his sense of insecurity!

Terrified, Don lay awake at nights, turning again and again to the Book at his bedside, and trying to pray. He needed God—that he knew. How could he hope to find Him other than through the Bible?

Tired out by sleepless nights Don would creep into an empty patient's bed during the day for a couple of stolen hours sleep—the only way he could keep going.

At last, Private Double's two-year national service stint came to an end. Don welcomed his 'demob' and his return to 'civvy street', and took a job on a fruit farm.

At this stage Don decided to attend the Congregational Church in which he had been brought up.

He especially appreciated 'Sailor's Sunday' when a Rev. Barkley from the Mission to Seamen preached. Mr Barkley gave a clear-cut Gospel message and told fascinating stories of sailors who had been converted.

The stories did something to Don and the preacher impressed him, but as yet he did not understand, and the inward ache increased.

Outwardly foul-mouthed and godless as ever, inwardly he pined for deliverance and for the God who made him. Such a heart cry would surely not go unheard.

One evening in October 1954 as Don returned from his day's work, he noticed some unusual posters plastered all over the town. They contained only the cryptic message, 'Peter Scothern is coming to Hadleigh!'

'Peter Scothern?' Don questioned his mother when he arrived home, 'Who is this fellow Peter Scothern?'

His mother turned from the stove where she was preparing the evening meal, and looked reflective for a moment. 'I don't know, I suppose he's one of those comedians on the radio, or something,' she offered.

When a second lot of posters put in their appearance, Don looked at them with great interest. Ah! These cleared up the mystery. There was to be an Evangelistic Crusade in the Hadleigh Town Hall. Moreover, they were going to pray for the sick! The poster featured a testimony concerning a little crippled girl who had been healed and could now walk. 'Medical evidence confirms the miracle,' the poster claimed!

What a laugh! This should be a bit of fun. Miracles of healing? Good grief! Impossible! If anything is really happening, it has to be a fake, he decided.

The next Sunday night Don came out of the Congregational Church after the evening service and strode deliberately across the road to get in on the fun.

He entered the Town Hall, with its big old-fashioned beams, to find the meeting place already moderately full. The platform where the speaker sat looked bright and attractive, decorated with chrysanthemums and crêpe paper. The song leader, enthusiastically leading the congregation in a catchy chorus, glanced approvingly at the new arrivals, as Don and a few others made their way in.

Don found a seat not too near the front and settled down to see what would happen. Something did happen—but it was to himself. He found the meeting electrifying. It was not anything particular that the preacher said, or even that the sick were prayed for—it was the atmosphere. The Presence of God seemed to be there.

When the meeting ended, Don felt reluctant to return home. He made his way out slowly, one desire alone possessing him—to get back down there again as soon as possible.

Monday night found him once more in the Town Hall. A good crowd had gathered and again they were singing that captivating chorus:

On Calvary's tree, He died for me
That I His love might know.
To set me free, He died for me,
That's why I love Him so.

Don glanced around. Many of those singing looked as if they really meant it. He began to join in. They repeated the chorus again and again. Not two or three times, but perhaps a dozen or even fifteen times. The words started to take a hold. Don began to feel almost as if he meant them too.

Next came a testimony. A young man, Vic Ramsey by name, came forward and told what Jesus Christ meant to him personally. What interested Don most was that this man had just been married. He had left his wife at Great Yarmouth sixty-odd miles away (where they were setting up house having just returned from their honeymoon) to be present at this meeting. For a man to do that, Don reasoned, he had to be in earnest. There must be reality in his experience of Christ.

Later in the service came the main message. Don could not recall afterwards the actual sermon preached —only the inspiration of that faith-charged atmosphere.

Then came the invitation. It was simple enough. No emotionalism or pressurizing.

'Now while every head is bowed and every eye closed I just want to ask you one question. As you have listened to the Word of God, I am sure that many of you have felt your own need of Jesus Christ. He is here by His Spirit waiting and longing to bless you. Are you willing to receive Him tonight as your Lord and your Saviour? Then please raise your right hand—now!'

Don needed no second urging. He stood to his feet, tall and erect. No half-mast hand-raising for a man with a burden as great as his. It was two minutes to nine, October 18, 1954.

Next, Evangelist Peter Scothern requested those receiving Christ to move forward to the front. Don went, followed by four or five other people.

Head bowed, he moved quickly, as if Jesus Christ Himself were standing there waiting for him—as indeed He was. Tears, the first in many years, streamed down his face, releasing the tensions and suppressed griefs of his chequered young life.

Ushered into chairs at the front, the new converts sat briefly while Mr Scothern prayed with them. They were then handed over to counsellors, and who should Don's counsellor be but the young man who had testified!

Vic Ramsey took hold of Don's hand in a friendly grip and shook it vigorously. 'Mr Double,' he said enthusiastically with something like excitement in his tone, 'Mr Double, it's a wonderful new life!'

Vic prayed with Don, taking him through a few Scriptures and encouraging him to read his Bible regularly. Then he game him his card with a warm and open invitation to visit his home.

Don says, 'I'm so glad he didn't say, "Look, here's a book of rules and regulations. From now on you must do this, and this. But make sure you don't do that. . ."'.

No, instead he told him with joy and conviction, 'It's a wonderful new life,' and Don in his simplicity believed him.

As Don walked home through the chilly night to his parents' house, he knew that something had happened.

He couldn't define it of course. He couldn't have told you in so many words, 'I've been born again.' He just knew he was a different man. He felt clean and happy.

God had forgiven his past. The present and the future rested in His hands. A new life had begun indeed—a Wonderful New Life.

Next day Don went as usual to his work on the fruit farm. At lunch time the boys gathered around him for the latest smutty story, but instead he hold them how the night before he had given his heart and life to Jesus Christ.

'Ha, Double's gone religious,' they guffawed. 'He's got the latest craze. We'll give him two weeks. He'll soon be back with us.'

But Don was different. No more rude stories. No more lies. He didn't curse or swear.

At the end of two weeks the boys said, 'We'll give him three months. He's sure to give it up sooner or later.'

'But,' says Don, 'at the end of three months they gave *me* up.' Even his mother, while marvelling at the change that had come over him, just could not believe that it would last. 'You'll never be able to keep it up,' she reasoned negatively.

She recalled wistfully the high expectations that had attended the birth of her only son. What bitter disappointments she had suffered since. What devious paths they were that had brought them all to this day.

With hope struggling against doubt, her mind swept back across the years.

2

A 'Double' Blessing

June 27, 1934 dawned grey and cold. Unseasonable fog veiled the small country town of Hadleigh in Suffolk, providing the local inhabitants with a handy topic of conversation. Grumbling good-naturedly to one another about the erratic English summer, they set about the business of the day.

But at least one family in Hadleigh had more important things on their minds that chilly morning than talk about the weather. For several hours the small semi-detached house in George Street had been alive with bustling activity and suppressed excitement.

Farm-hand George Double had been up since 1 a.m. For some time had had been pacing the room in classic fashion. Now he glanced nervously at the clock for the umpteenth time. Nearly 6 a.m. Seconds later the door clicked open and a kindly middle-aged woman appeared carrying an animated bundle. George's face relaxed into its usual mild lines and his eyes came alight with joy.

'Well, Mr Double,' the midwife announced cheerfully, 'you have a fine boy. Look at his weight!'

At eleven pounds, perhaps we may say that Donald Hamilton Double made an 'abundant entrance' into this world. Certainly there could scarcely have been a more welcome child anywhere.

For Lilian and George Double, the birth of a son was

13

the culmination of much waiting and agonizing. Ever since the death six years before of their tiny premature daughter Josephine Joan, aged thirteen days, they had envisaged such a day as this, praying in anticipation and longing, 'Oh God, let this one live.'

In the days and months that followed Don's birth, an array of doting parents, grandparents and aunts surrounded the small boy. If they tended to give the impression that the beguiling imp who lived at number 31 was someone rather special, you have to remember that it is not everyone's baby who wins first prize at the local baby show.

As the chubby curly-haired boy grew, delighting his Mum and Dad with his childish prattle, or making them dizzy as he drove his three-wheeler bike round and round the kitchen table, how could they guess that ominous clouds were gathering over their happy home?

Unfortunately the two-bedroomed house in George Street where Don first saw the light of day, and where he spent the first four years of his life, held an unhappy secret.

Ten years previously it had been the scene of the death of a woman suffering from tuberculosis. Although the house had been thoroughly cleaned and redecorated, it seems that somewhere hidden in the masonry lurked the treacherous bacillus that was to play havoc with Don's childhood and which robbed him of the better part of his school days.

When Don reached his fifth year the family finally moved into the High Street, opposite the police station. But by that time, although unknown to them, the damage was already done.

3

Satan's Punch Bag

About the time the Doubles moved house, Aunt Gladys began to take young Don to Sunday School, which practice she continued whenever possible throughout his childhood days.

The Doubles were nominally 'Congregational', although Lilian Double had formerly been a Methodist, and at the age of thirteen had experienced conversion. Looking back now to her youth and early married life she says, 'But I didn't know the Lord then, as I know Him now.'

George Double too was just a nominal Christian, only coming into a personal knowledge of Jesus Christ at a much later date, following his son's conversion.

September 1939 brought changes into the home in the High Street. The first event of significance—Don started school. Proud and happy in his new silk suit, curly mop well brushed, every hair temporarily in place, he hopefully began his formal education.

The second event of importance that momentous year was of course the outbreak of World War II, and it wasn't long before air-raid warnings became the order of the day.

Each time the long eerie undulating siren began its wail, Lilian Double and neighbouring mothers would rush to the school in Threadneedle Street to bring home their young. Then they would retire to the safest place available, which for young Donald and his parents was the large hall in the centre of the house.

But this was only the beginning of trouble for the Double household. A painful and unsightly swelling began to appear on the right side of their son's neck.

The local doctor first diagnosed it as mumps, but the child's continuing listlessness, and the fact that the lump didn't go away, led them to make the ten-mile trip to the Ipswich and East Suffolk Hospital for tests and a more expert opinion.

After the inevitable long hours of waiting, tests and more waiting, the doctor at last called them in and acquainted Lilian Double with his diagnosis—a tubercular gland.

'I'm sorry, Mrs Double,' he informed her quietly in a voice calculated not to alarm, 'We'll have to take him into hospital right away.'

But the doctor's kind concern was lost on the stunned listener. He might just as well have been a judge delivering a heavy sentence, for in those days before the advent of our modern wonder drugs, the word 'tuberculosis' had a particularly ominous sound. Fear twisted in Lilian Double's heart. Feeling trapped and alarmed, she knew that she had no alternative other than to consent to the hospitalization of her small son.

Following a few formalities, a trim young nurse led the little fellow away, his piercing screams echoing down the long white corridors.

Lilian Double made her way to the door in a daze. Outside she could still hear the heart-rending cries of her small boy, a sound which haunted her many times throughout the anxious weeks that followed.

Don took a long time to settle down, perhaps because in those somewhat sterner days no parental visits were allowed, the motive of course being to minimize upsets. The actual result in the case of young children seemed to be that after the first traumatic week or two they virtually forgot their parents. So it was in Don's case.

Visiting being restricted to their minister the Rev. Pearce, he kindly reported back regularly to the family. At least he could pass on those little tit-bits of news that worried parents need to hear. Direct phone enquiries produced little more than the official 'comfortable', which always left them feeling more helpless and alone than ever.

As for the child, his home was now the balcony of the children's ward, where he could be nursed in the fresh air.

Following an operation he lay swathed in bandages which covered the whole of his head, only his bewildered blue eyes being visible as they peered out upon a world suddenly gone topsy-turvy.

His neck needed constant attention and dressing. They had put in yards of gauze 'draining' and Don particularly remembers the kind gentle specialist surgeon Dr Hill, who encouraged him when they removed the draining by telling him, 'You're a very brave boy.'

While little Don's private war with sickness and change was being waged inside the children's ward in Ipswich, the 1940 blitz continued unabated in the country at large.

One night stands out above the others in the memories of the Double family. The sirens had sounded. George and Lilian Double could see the flares falling over Ipswich, and could hear the bombs exploding as they paced the garden in an agony of mind.

Being a major port, Ipswich, the county town of Suffolk, was a favourite target for the bombers; the docks, located about one mile from the hospital, being the main object of attack. In point of fact, not a few of the bombs fell on the residential areas; and on the night in question many actually fell in Park Street, right behind the Ipswich and East Suffolk General.

Within the hospital itself there must have been fear in many hearts, but the hospital staff went about their duties with calm control. The raiders made some devastating hits that night, and one small boy remembers to this day the noise of the blasts and the terrifying vibrations, as the whole place shook again and again.

As he sobbed with fear, trying to hide his face in the pillow, he felt a touch on his shoulder. He looked up. It was the night nurse who had just come on duty.

'Don't worry, Donnie,' she soothed. 'You don't need to be afraid. Jesus is looking after us. Jesus doesn't allow the Germans to bomb hospitals, you know.'

Don had heard a little about Jesus in Sunday School. He knew He was the Friend of little children. Now, as the unknown nurse made this practical application of her own faith, Don had his first lesson in trust. He accepted her word, found great comfort in the knowledge of a God who cares, and after a short while fell fast asleep.

A new day dawned over the smoking devastation of the city. George and Lilian Double phoned as early as they dared and learnt with relief and thankfulness that all was well within the confines of the hospital.

Five long weeks passed. Not once had Don's parents had so much as a glimpse of him. Now they decided to enquire if perhaps they might be allowed to see him even through a window, without his seeing them. To their joy, they were informed that they could come and take him home.

Eagerly they came to collect him. For Don's part he had become quite attached to the other children and his cheerful nurses, and seemed quite apathetic about the prospect of returning home.

'It's nice here. You get good food,' he responded unemotionally as his mother removed the ill-fitting hospital pyjamas and dressed him in his own clothes.

Don soon settled into life at home again, but the once healthy little boy was now a weak and sickly child. The next few years of his life were to be dominated by visits to the hospital as an outpatient—three times a week at first, and later once a week.

The ten-mile journey by bus was always a trial. Due to wartime shortage of fuel, the Eastern Counties' buses ran on a gas which gave off an unpleasant smell. This used to make Don feel very ill and by the time they reached the hospital, he was often violently sick.

Later Don had to be hospitalized for a few days, for the removal of his tonsils. One morning he had the surprise of his life. He looked up from his bed to see a window cleaner appearing up the ladder and signalling to him through the window. He was overjoyed. 'Coo,' he exulted proudly to anyone who cared to listen, 'It's my Dad!' Mr Double cleaned the hospital windows from time to time on a voluntary basis. Hence his unheralded appearance.

A second outbreak of the tubercular gland some time later involved yet more outpatient attendance and a sort of electrical treatment which produced a very unpleasant reaction.

During those turbulent years Don saw little of the inside of a school room. For a while he was wheeled about for walks in the pleasant Suffolk countryside, and in the park. Later as he grew a little stronger he would play for hours, weather permitting, in their spacious garden with its beautiful lawn.

Although Don had few companions his own age, he was not really lonely. He had many animal friends, including pigs, chickens and rabbits, which he loved and enjoyed looking after. He would get the rabbits out of their hutches and play with them on the lawn.

There were also fresh fruits and vegetables straight

from the garden to be enjoyed. Even today there is nothing he likes better than a big plateful of garden vegetables full of flavour, freshly picked and cooked immediately.

Milk of course was another must in those days, not to mention cod-liver-oil (ghastly stuff!). But according to Don's mother he never made a fuss.

In spite of bits and pieces of spelling and other work sent from the school, Don found it virtually impossible to make any progress in the three R's. Having missed out on the basics of his education he hardly knew how to apply himself to study, and with no trained teacher to assist him, he went through his childhood unable to read or write.

Consequently, he developed what he describes as 'a whacking great inferiority complex'. This lasted through into his adult life, until he finally found deliverance from it, by the power of Jesus Christ.

By the time Don reached eleven years he had grown tall and thin. He began to attend school a little during the warmer months of the year, but recurring bronchitis kept him home for long periods during the winter.

Those years were hardly happy ones for the lonely lad. He stood out like Tokyo Tower among his peers, being conspicuous both for his height and for his illiteracy, which the local kids mistakenly interpreted as stupidity. They continually beat him up and knocked him down. 'I was used as a punch-bag,' he comments.

Whether or not Satan has any degree of foreknowledge we cannot be sure; but it does seem as if he took great delight in battering, both body and soul, a lad destined in days to come to be mightily used of God in the salvation and healing of multitudes.

One thing in which Don did begin to excel as he grew older and stronger was sports. He loved football and cricket. Selected to play in the school cricket team, his delight knew no bounds.

Being a born enthusiast he would also cycle four miles to Elmsett each Saturday, where he reputedly hit the ball with such gusto that it was not unheard of for him to break the bat!

He also recalls blissful visits to an uncle and aunt in Cambridge whenever a touring team came to the city to play the University. Then he would spend whole days at the Fenners just watching the play. Happy days indeed.

Don also joined the cubs, and later the scouts, where he earned a whole sleeveful of badges and learned to play the big drum in the scout band. At his first actual parade he felt so tense that he held the drum sticks too tightly. By the end of the parade his fingers were raw and painful where the skin had been rubbed off.

The annual Scout Gang Shows were great fun. On one occasion Don acted the part of a woman. Beautifully fitted out complete with bonnet and powder and lipstick, he brought the house down with his performance as a proponent of 'women's lib' on a soap box in Hyde Park.

Incidentally, he makes it clear that his support of 'women's lib' was purely temporary! However, Don is all in favour of that true liberation of spirit, wherewith Christ can set us free—both men and women.

Throughout most of Don's childhood he continued, when well enough, to attend both Sunday School and church. He says, 'I even sang in the choir,' which comment always raises a laugh, for Don cannot carry a tune even to this day, though he does delight in making a 'joyful noise' to the Lord!

Unfortunately, there was not much spiritual life in the church as a whole, and the growing lad grew restless and bored. After all, is anything more insipid than a formal Christianity which has only an historical Christ, and knows nothing of the exciting, vital Jesus who still lives today?

Yet in spite of the general torpor, one Sunday School teacher stands out in Don's memory as a true Christian. Week by week he sowed Gospel truth in the hearts of inattentive little boys, who fooled around and pulled his leg unmercifully. What if a seed was to lie dormant for a while like a hidden, unexploded bomb? Some day God would detonate it, setting a soul on fire.

Meanwhile, Don lost all interest in religious activity; and by the time he left school at the age of fifteen he hailed the occasion as his opportunity to graduate from church attendance.

4

'Remember Not the Sins of My Youth'

Don's first job after leaving school lasted exactly four weeks! Expecting to train as an electrician, he started work in a radio shop, earning £1.25 per week.

Unfortunately one of his tasks as junior involved handling the old-fashioned accumulators; putting them on charge and taking them off again. This made him feel so ill that he could not carry on. Regretfully he terminated his apprenticeship.

Taking a temporary job, Don now picked fruit for a couple of months, his £2 pay-packet burning in his pocket as he walked home proudly after his first 47-hour week.

Summer ended, Don's next venture into the adult world of industry and commerce led him to a Wine and Spirit Merchant in Ipswich, which seemed to set the tone for his teenage years. For £1.75 per week, he now spent two days a week corking and labelling newly bottled *Guinness*, and the other three days washing empty bottles.

Engaged in this uninspiring occupation by day, Don began to spend his evenings at a Social Club where he whiled away long hours playing snooker, and sometimes table tennis. There, along with the other lads, he learnt to smoke, and drink, and swear; anything to look big and be 'in' with the boys—anything in fact to combat the terrible feeling of inferiority which oppressed him continually.

Behind the young lad's studied façade of 'bigness' cringed a heart full of fears and self-doubt. His lack of learning, coupled with acute self-consciousness about the ugly scar on his neck, weighed heavily on his spirit.

To this we may add his fear of being alone, his fear of the dark, fear of water, fear of dogs. No wonder Don felt fate had been particularly malicious towards him, and unconsciously reacted with frustrated fury.

Recalling those unhappy days Don says, 'I swore and cursed with every sentence I spoke, no matter who was present.'

He also excelled in collecting vulgar jokes. These gave him a dubious popularity with his work-mates as they gathered round him at the morning tea-break for the latest filth.

Most of his wages he spent on drink. Somehow he managed to hide his drinking habits from his parents, creeping through their bedroom late at night, into his own, on many a wild weekend.

The arrival of Don's National Service papers following his eighteenth birthday was a blessing in disguise. While it is true that his conduct went from bad to worse during his two years in the army, at least it rescued him from the unsavoury backwater of beer and bottles as a means of daily employment, and launched him out again into mid-stream.

At his first medical, the army turned him down on the basis of his past health record. Then someone must have had second thoughts, for they called him back for another opinion, passing him A 1.

The ten-week initial training period in the R.A.M.C. proved to be a great shock to Don's system, as to many another wayward teenager. But he survived, and even grew to quite enjoy army life.

The first night in camp Don's eyes boggled to see one

24

young soldier kneel and pray before getting into bed. This the lad continued to do regularly, and while Don roared with laughter along with the rest, secretly he admired him.

The Christian soldier from Swindon, Wiltshire, who referred to himself as 'an evangelical', seemed to carry with him an aura of peace, which comforted Don— giving him a vicarious sense of security, so that he even experienced regret when their ways parted.

Because of Don's height, they now made him a regimental policeman, and sent him to the large barracks at Crookham, near Fleet, Hampshire.

When they came to fit him with his uniform, the longest trousers on hand seemed to come halfway up his calf! The quartermaster looked in dismay at Don's 6-foot-5½-inch frame. 'A disgrace to the British Army,' he pronounced. 'Don't you go outside the barracks until we get some made to measure.'

But clothing was not the only problem. Where could they find a bed to fit him? Nowhere! But then tall men have to learn to live with such small discomforts.

Throughout those grey teenage years, one bright spot which cheered Don's existence centred around an attractive young lady with dark brown hair.

He first met her in Christ Church Park, while hanging around with the crowd looking for some action. Taken with her coquettish ways, the sixteen-year-old lad felt flattered when she agreed to see him again.

Don kept company with her for more than three years, shutting his eyes to the trouble signs which appeared from time to time.

On several occasions during the months immediately prior to their marriage, she went around with other fellows, telling him about it after the event. Then, fearful that neither she, nor any other girl for that matter, would stick by him, Don spent long hours trying to convince her that he was the one she really loved—not those other freaks, and virtually talked her into marrying him.

The young lady's mother wisely opposed the union, but the couple, both still under twenty-one years, sought court permission to marry. And the law, which apparently cares little for the scriptural injunction, 'Children, obey your parents . . .' issued the desired permit.

On April 10th, 1954 the marriage was solemnized in the Hadleigh Congregational Church; and not realizing the trouble and sorrow that lay in its wake, the immature young man, resplendent in his military uniform, led his bride triumphantly down the aisle.

This marriage was later dissolved following repeated acts of infidelity by Don's wife. But he hopes that the heartbreak and suffering he experienced during that period may be a warning to others not to fall into the same trap. 'There must be genuine love and a scriptural yoking together in accordance with God's Word for there to be a proper foundation for a successful marriage,' he insists.

Shortly before Don's 'demob', he put in an application to the police force, hoping to go straight into it when he left the Army. Alas for the hope! The entrance exam involved writing an essay. When Don's papers were returned to him, they had changed colour! Red ink practically obliterated the blue ink with its atrocious spelling. Utter failure!

Don swallowed his pride, squared his shoulders, and took a full-time job at Cook's fruit farm.

This, then, was the situation at the time of his conversion.

5

Kept by the Power of God

After Don's transforming experience in the Hadleigh Town Hall, life fell back into its familiar patterns—but with this difference: the ache had gone. He no longer walked alone.

Cycling the two miles to and from his work each day, Don spent much time conversing with his new Friend, delighting in the sense of His presence. He enjoyed the outdoor life on the farm too, taking a keen interest in his work, which offered quite a bit of variety depending on the season of the year.

As he pruned apple trees in the winter of 1954, Don had plenty of time to muse upon the tremendous change in his outlook. God had become to him 'Someone Very Great', bigger than he could really comprehend. He felt he wanted the whole world to know about Him.

Don tried to talk to the boys about the Lord, but for the most part, they just didn't want to know, regarding the whole thing as a huge joke.

On one occasion when one of his work mates tried to disprove the existence of God, Don told him of the healing power of Jesus and of the miracles he had witnessed at the meetings.

'I even saw a cross-eyed woman healed,' Don related.

'Okay,' said his friend, 'I've got a headache right now. Ask God to take it away from me.'

Don wilted. But only for a moment. Taking up the gauntlet he placed his hand on his pal's shoulder and prayed sheepishly, 'Please Lord, heal Bill's headache and help him to believe in you.' Wonder of wonders—the headache went.

There is evidence that the young man became an instant convert, and the incident certainly boosted Don's own faith up a notch or two. Don also had reason in those early months of his Christian life to prove the Lord's healing power for his own body.

While still in the army, two doctors had diagnosed an anal fissure, and assured him that the only cure would be a surgical operation. Now the trouble flared up again.

Don went to the local doctor, who confirmed the diagnosis and confirmed the need for surgery. He promptly made an appointment for Don to be seen by a surgeon, with a view to an immediate operation.

The night before Don was due to appear at the hospital, he knelt by his bedside and prayed. His request was simple, but his trust implicit. 'Lord,' he began, 'you healed the people in that crusade. Lord, I'm sick. I don't want an operation. Will you please heal me? Thank you, Jesus. Amen.'

By next morning the pain had gone, and Don had stopped passing blood. His visit to the hospital turned out to be a humiliating farce.

The eminent surgeon, gloved and gowned, examined him with a puzzled expression on his face.

'Anal fissure? There's no sign of an anal fissure here, young man. Nothing wrong with you, Mr Double.'

Turning away in disgust, the surgeon quickly removed his rubber gloves, tossed them into a kidney dish, and washed his hands. Then before Don, flushed with embarrassment, could stammer out any word of explanation, he passed him over to a young intern and,

28

muttering darkly about the inefficiency of private practicioners, strode from the room.

Don left the hospital with feelings of mortification still washing over him. But he could see the funny side of the incident too. Chuckling a little as he gave thanks to God, his faith seemed to be turning cartwheels as he made his way home.

About this time, Don moved out of his parents' home, into a small place on a £400 mortgage. An old terraced dwelling with a winding, rickety staircase, it boasted four rooms, an outside toilet, and a wash-house which he soon converted into a bathroom. The front walls of the house were damp, and in wet weather ran with water. No, it was not exactly a palace, but it was home—the first he had owned.

A further highlight in Don's life, the following spring, was the birth of a little son, followed later by a precious daughter. How proud and happy Don felt as each was placed in his arms for the first time—a son and a daughter to bring up for the Lord.

But there were barren places in Don's experience during that first year of his Christian life. He had continued to attend the local Congregational Church on Sundays, but sadly lacked any solid diet of Bible teaching. Consequently, he did not grow much in the knowledge of his new found faith. Don tried to read his Bible but without much success. He could hardly spell his own name and address, let alone read.

Then something happened that changed the whole picture. Peter Scothern returned to Hadleigh for a follow-up crusade.

Twelve months had passed since Don's conversion. Now as he stepped back into the stimulating atmosphere of an evangelistic meeting—this time not as an unbeliever but as a Christian, everything seemed to come alive and fall into place.

The first evening when they asked for brief testimonies, Don rose to his feet and shared in a few hesitant words something of what God had done in his life.

He also became a candidate for water baptism and although at that time did not fully comprehend its symbolism—identification with Christ in His death, burial, and resurrection—yet the occasion marked a definite point in Don's spiritual experience.

'Baptism is not a trivial or optional extra,' Don explains. 'God never asks us to do optional things. Everything He requires has a purpose.'

He now began to attend some meetings in the home of the Rev. David Rushworth Smith.

Mr Smith was minister of a daughter church of the Hadleigh Congregational Church and had been the one responsible for inviting Peter Scothern to Hadleigh in the first place.

At the first house meeting, to his surprise, Don found himself praying aloud in public. He stuttered and stumbled a bit, but what did that matter? The prayer was for God, not for man.

His Bible studies too opened up new vistas to Don's eager spirit, and his faith found firm support, as like a hungry bird seeking nourishment it came to settle upon the solid foundation of the Word of God.

From this time onwards the pace of Don's spiritual life accelerated. 'It appears that I began to run with God,' he says, 'instead of merely ambling.'

6

God Specializes in 'Failures'

As Don began to move forward in his Christian life, he became conscious of a growing desire to serve the Lord. At the same time, he could not help but be aware of his many inabilities and insufficiencies.

What could he do—a man without even the rudiments of education? How could he ever amount to anything in the kingdom of God? The word 'failure' seemed to stand out starkly over much of his life.

As agonies such as these plagued Don increasingly, some of the joy began to drain out of his Christian experience. Yet, surely, there must be an answer. He sought out his pastor acquaintance David Rushworth Smith.

Slim, wavy-haired, very correctly dressed, looking every inch the minister, Mr Smith ushered Don into his living room. Don felt uncouth by contrast, as towering above him he stretched out his hands in a gesture half despairing, half hopeful.

'Look,' he began. 'Look pastor, you and the others are always talking about miracles. Tell me. Do you think that God could give me an education?' There! It was out!

David Smith regarded Don thoughtfully. 'Well,' he replied, motioning for him to sit down. 'It really depends on what you want it for. If you want to do something for the Lord and work for Him, then you need to be filled with the Holy Spirit.'

Pastor Smith had been fingering his Bible as he spoke. Now he opened it, leafing rapidly through the pages till he came to the book of Acts, chapter 4. He held it out for Don to see, pointing to verse 13 as he did so.

'Look Don. The Bible says that Peter and John were unlearned and ignorant men. Yet when they were filled with the Holy Ghost, they were some of those whom God used to turn the world upside down.'

He laid the Bible down and looked at Don intently. 'If you get filled with the Holy Spirit, unlearned and ignorant as you are, you'll have all you need to work for God.'

'Fair enough,' replied Don. 'Then that's what I want. I want to be filled with the Holy Ghost.'

A week or two later after further prayer and heart preparation, Don went into Ipswich where Pastor Smith was conducting an evangelistic crusade. After the meeting several of Don's friends gathered around as Mr Smith laid hands on him and prayed for him to receive the fullness of the Spirit.

Following the prayer everyone assured Don that he had now been filled. Encouraged, he tried for the next six months to believe it. But there was little change in his situation. The whole experience had been altogether too abstract.

The following months, however, brought other changes into Don's life that he had not envisaged. Although continuing to work at Cook's Fruit Farm, he also began to learn the fish-and-chip trade, and was soon relieving the local fried-fish shop owner four evenings a week.

Don so enjoyed this occupation that before long he made application to become the manager of a fish-and-chip shop belonging to the Ipswich Co-operative Society.

Acceptance for the position entailed moving from Hadleigh to the city, but included a pleasant roomy flat over the Co-op shop in Bramford Lane.

Virtually his own boss, Don made innovations and trade increased. He also found ample opportunity to put in a word for the Lord over the counter as he scooped crisp, batter-covered mouth-watering fish and piping hot chips into grease-proof bags; salting and vinegaring them with typical Double enthusiasm.

Meanwhile, in the plan of God, David Rushworth Smith had also moved to Ipswich, having temporarily left the Congregational Church. Here the minister recommended his weekly meetings for prayer and Bible study, choosing Monday evenings to fit in with Don's one free week-night. These gatherings, held in a local hall, became known as the Ipswich Revival Fellowship.

Don also began to attend the Elim Church on Sundays, where besides forming some new and vital friendships, he established several more 'firsts' in his Christian experience.

It was here that he gave his first real tesimony. Not a planned or premeditated one, in the safe company of the saints, but in the open air, in the very area where he had formerly fooled around with the boys.

As they set up their loudspeaker that evening at the old cattle market near the main bus stop, Don's eyes wandered casually over the potential congregation.

He noted with satisfaction the presence of several familiar faces among the milling crowd. 'They surely need the message,' he reflected. 'I'm glad we have some good preachers with us tonight.'

The first hymn now being ended, the Rev. Sainsbury stood in the middle of the ring and introduced the first speaker. 'We have here with us this evening a young man whom I'm sure many of you will know.'

Don glanced about him curiously, vaguely wondering

to whom the minister could be referring.

'About eighteen months ago,' the pastor continued, 'God met with this young man in a very definite way and changed his life completely. But now, I mustn't steal his thunder must I? Come along Don. Come and tell the folk what Jesus Christ has done for you.'

Motioning a flabbergasted Don to the microphone, the minister stepped back leaving him holding the field.

All eyes fastened on the lean young giant. Here and there among the crowd a derisive grin spread across a face or two. Don gulped, sent up an S.O.S. prayer, opened his mouth and began. Words tumbled out— earnestly, urgently. What he lacked in polish he made up for in sincerity. And no one listening could doubt that to Don Double at least, Jesus Christ was a present-tense reality.

Another milestone in Don's experience concerned the winning of his first two souls, his friends Dennis Wakeling and wife.

Don invited them along to some evangelistic meetings at the church and his joy knew no bounds when they both gave their hearts to the Lord.

But in spite of these victories, when the thrill wore off Don experienced times of real depression. Still frustrated by a sense of failure and inferiority, his needs were real. He began to get desperate. There just had to be something more.

Whenever work or family permitted, Don escaped to his room where he locked the door and poured out his heart to God, pleading that He would baptize him in the Holy Spirit as He did His early disciples.

Don does not believe that such agonizing is an indispensable requisite to receiving the baptism in the Holy Spirit. God deals with each person differently. But this seemed to be the way Don had to come.

Finally, God spoke to him. Not in an audible voice,

yet with a clarity there could be no mistaking. 'October 20th.'

Startled, Don rose from his knees and looked at the calendar. October 20th! That date seemed to ring a bell. Hastily he pulled some papers out of a drawer, thumbing through them until he came to the one he sought—Peter Scothern's itinerary.

There it was! Peter Scothern was scheduled to speak at the Ipswich Elim Church on that date. Hallelujah, that was going to be his day!

Saturday October 20th, 1956 arrived. Expectant and determined, Don set out for the evening meeting. 'Lord, I'm going to get filled with the Holy Spirit if I have to stay there till Communion Service tomorrow morning. Lord, I'm not going home until you baptize me in the Holy Spirit.'

They had a great meeting that night. A number of souls were saved. Miracles of healing took place. Finally, the preacher announced the benediction.

Why, he hadn't even mentioned the baptism in the Holy Spirit! Don felt cheated. 'He's not going to get away with that,' he said to himself desperately. He waited for Evangelist Scothern to pronounce the final 'Amen', then sprinted down the aisle like an Olympic star doing the hundred yard dash.

'I pinned him at the front near the piano,' Don recalls. 'Brother,' he pleaded, 'I want to receive the baptism in the Holy Spirit.'

Peter Scothern looked at Don for a moment, then pointed to the front row of chairs, 'Get down there and receive it then,' he expostulated. With that, he turned and walked away, greeting some other friends who were waiting their turn to speak with him.

Don knew now how Naaman the Syrian must have felt when Elisha, instead of ministering to him directly, sent his servant out with a message to dip in Jordan seven times.

Talk about anti-climax! Don had at least expected the laying on of hands. Perhaps a bit of shouting, or some other Pentecostal-type ritual. Instead, this fellow said, 'Get down there and receive it then,' and as Don went one way, he went another.

'Lord,' Don breathed sinking to his knees. Then it happened! No sooner had his knees touched the floor than the power of the Holy Spirit fell upon him.

Don has no recollection that up to that time he had ever heard anyone speak in tongues. But now he felt himself vibrating within. Caught up in the presence and power of God he found himself giving utterance to a strange language, praising and extolling the Lord as the disciples of Jesus had done on the day of Pentecost.

Several persons making their way out, turned and gazed curiously. Others who understood what was going on began to praise God and rejoice with him.

Don comments, 'Something happened to me that night. Some people reckon that the baptism in the Spirit and speaking in tongues are of the devil. Well, if that is the case, I can only say that the devil must have got converted, for the baptism in the Spirit made Jesus more real. And the cross became more wonderful than ever before.'

Next day, still aglow with the Spirit's presence, as Don knelt in prayer he heard the Lord telling him, 'I'm calling you to be an evangelist. You are to go and preach the Gospel in the small towns and villages. . . .'

God has spoken to Don on various occasions since then—a still small voice not audible to the outward ear, but so clear as to leave no room for doubt.

'I know when God has spoken to me in this outstanding way,' Don says, 'It is so clear I'd stake my life on it. I don't need any confirmation.'

Now God had told him, 'I'm calling you to be an

evangelist.'

Next evening being Monday, Don rushed down to the Ipswich Revival Fellowship thrilled and excited, anxious to share his good news.

'God has called me to the ministry,' he informed his friends ecstatically. Blank faces greeted his announcement.

'You?'

'You can't read or write.'

'You can't spell.'

'You could never go to Bible School and study.'

One after another the objections poured out, beating upon Don's spirit with the destructive potential of a hail storm on a field of ripened grain.

Unfortunately, as Don well knew, they were so right! How could he go to Bible School? How could he study, or produce coherent sermons and evangelistic messages? Yet surely that was God's problem. Not man's.

David Rushworth Smith said little. He neither encouraged nor discouraged, but looked on cautiously taking an 'I'll wait and see' attitude, as did several others of the more mature Christians.

For the next three months Don fought discouragement as he listened to the negative talk around him. Now and then he surfaced briefly, only to be shot down again by the next barrage.

Deep down in his heart he knew that God's call was real. He felt at Jeremiah did when he wrote, 'But his word was in mine heart as a burning fire shut up in my bones, and I was weary with forbearing and I could not stay' (Jeremiah 20:9).

At last he could stand it no longer. Don went down to the nearest village and booked a public hall.

With the help of two or three of his less incredulous friends, he duplicated a few handbills, and together they put them through the doors.

The following Saturday they had an evangelistic meeting. It was not a large gathering, but at the end twenty or more people were kneeling at the front, receiving Christ as their Saviour.

Don doesn't remember the content of the sermon he preached that night. One deep impression only remains. He received then the only credentials he would ever need to be an evangelist. God had confirmed his calling, bringing souls to new birth under his ministry.

As Don became increasingly involved in Christian activities, he found his work as manager of the Co-op Store too restrictive. He just had to have his evenings free. Consequently, he handed in his resignation.

He now took a position as a representative of Kleen-Eze Brushes, where many of the staff were active Christians, including the leading salesman. Don made good use of his door-to-door contacts, never forgetting that above all he was a representative of Jesus Christ.

Don could now work whatever hours he wished, which was most convenient. But of course he had to move out of his comfortable flat, and be content for a while with a house designated by the city council, in a very poor part of the town.

After about a year with Kleen-Eze, Don became a salesman on the staff of W. A. Turner Ltd. of Stowmarket, Suffolk, where his boss was a member of the Exclusive Brethren, and the general manager an elder in a Pentecostal Church.

Don's job now consisted of taking wholesale orders for sausages, pies and cooked meats.

At the time he joined the firm there were sixteen salesmen including himself, Don being the only Christian among them. Out of the sixteen journeys, he was given the one, second from the bottom, which only took about £240 in orders per week.

Now Don believed, and still does, that one of the best

ways to witness for the Lord is to excel in one's work. 'Any old thing' will not do from a Christian. 'Any old how' will not do for God. Our lives and work must tally with what we say.

So Don prayed, 'Lord, they have given me one of the worst journeys. It's just got to become the best—for I am a Christian. Lord, I'm looking to you to do it.' Thus Don took Jesus Christ as his partner in the work. 'And,' he stresses, 'I let Him be the senior partner.'

Because Don could not spell, he would look at the name over a shop and copy it before entering, so that he could write out his bills.

He prayed before going into each place, and praised the Lord for every order he received as he came out. Sometimes customers standing by would look up in amazement at Don's uninhibited 'Hallelujah, praise the Lord,' as he left the shop.

Within a month Don's orders had doubled: the journey now took £480 worth of orders per week. Before he left the firm to go into evangelism full time three years later, the journey had broken all records, topping £1088 in one week; the next best being around the £700 mark. Don gave all the praise where it belonged, for he knew he could never have done it on his own. His Senior Partner had directed operations.

The Lord also vindicated him among his unbelieving workmates. The first Christmas, they held a raffle in the canteen on a Saturday morning. When Don declined to buy a ticket, explaining politely, 'No thanks, I'm a Christian,' the men began to hoot and jeer.

The foreman, although not a believer himself, knew something of Don's record and regarded him highly.

'Don't you dare to laugh at him,' he intervened. 'He's got more back-bone than the lot of you.'

The laughter changed to sheepish silence, and from then on Don's Christian witness was held in respect.

7

Nana Williams—The Discipler

During those early years of Don's Christian experience, one of the most moulding and powerful influences seems to have been the friendship and prayers of an elderly lady, affectionately known as Nana Williams.

Already well into her sixties when Don first met her, Mrs Williams was the widow of an army man. Living alone in a two-roomed apartment in Norwich Road, Ipswich she subsisted frugally on her widow's pension, from which she also gave generously to the Lord's work. She even sacrificed her one little luxury—a tin of fruit and cream on Sundays, so that she could give the price of it to missionaries.

Don visited her two or three times a week, sometimes more, and could always count on her encouragement and prayers. 'I've never known anyone in all my Christian life who believed and practised prayer like Nana Williams did,' he says.

One of Don's earliest memories of this lady concerns the episode of his learning to drive a car. While still in Hadleigh, he had bought an old crate of a motor cycle, which nearly gave his poor mother a nervous break-down every time she saw him on it. His father eventually persuaded him to get rid of it, promising to treat him to some driving lessons at the British School of Motoring. Don agreed.

As the time of his test drew near, Don began to feel

uneasy. A large percentage of learner drivers failed the first test. To top it all, his instructor assured him that he would certainly not pass if his two major weaknesses— failure to look in his mirror before signalling, and his three-point-turn—became evident during the test.

Would he make it? Don visited Nana Williams and shared his anxiety.

Nana took the burden as her own, and enlisting the support of another prayer warrior, Sister Rose Chapman, promised that they would both be on their knees praying during the crucial hour of the examination.

Bolstered by the knowledge of such support, Don's morale rose like a rocket at lift-off. Sitting behind the wheel with the examiner at his side, he lifted his heart to the Lord in silent prayer. 'Lord,' he breathed, 'I refuse to drive this car. I believe you to drive it through me.'

The test went without a hitch and Don passed with flying colours, for as he himself says, 'The Lord Jesus has never failed a driving test, or any other test either. Hallelujah.'

Don now made a point of driving Nana Williams to and from meetings, and took her out for a drive most Sunday afternoons. He never regarded these kindnesses to an old lady as a sacrifice. On the contrary, he gained more than he gave as she shared with him her long experience of God's dealings and faithfulness. Listening to her loving, yet authoritative voice, he felt faith being built into him—a faith that would stand him in good stead in the coming days.

How could he ever forget her fascinating stories of the Lord's provision? Nana would often go out witnessing on the streets, returning to find that someone had filled her coal bunker, or left a box of groceries on her doorstep.

One Sunday a car load of friends dropped in unexpectedly just about tea time. All she had available to feed them with was the remains of a small loaf of bread, and her views on Sunday observance being rigid, she had no intention of going out to buy anything.

What should she do? Apologize to her friends, explaining that she had nothing to offer them? They would surely have understood. But no, Nana Williams believed that if God had sent the visitors, He would also make provision for them.

She laid her hands over the diminutive loaf-end, closing her eyes, but lifting her head. 'Lord,' she said boldly, 'I want you to multiply this bread, as you did the loaves and fishes in Galilee. In Jesus' name. Amen.'

With that she picked up the butter knife, spread a slice and cut it, placing it on the large bread plate which she only brought out when visitors came. Then she spread another, then another, then another. On and on she cut until the plate brimmed with delicious looking fare. Without turning a hair, Nana wrapped up the remaining bread which still retained its original size, and put it away carefully in the bread-bin to be used for her supper.

Joyfully she picked up her plate of miracle bread, and took it in to her guests, serving them matter of factly as if nothing unusual had taken place.

Then there was the occasion when Don turned up at Nana's house just as a delivery man was coming out of the gate. Seeing a bulky looking parcel on Nana's kitchen table, Don smiled and said, 'It looks like you're having an early Christmas.'

Nana's eyes twinkled merrily, 'In God's kingdom it's Christmas all the year round', she observed. 'Look at the label, Don.'

Don looked. The parcel had been delivered from a large departmental store. It read: 'From the Lord Jesus

Christ.'

Exuberantly, they opened the parcel together, but Nana did not really seem surprised when she found a beautiful new coat inside. After all, she had been praying for one. She gazed at it for some minutes, until Don grew almost impatient.

'Aren't you going to try it on and see if it fits?' he urged.

'See if it fits, Don?' Nana reproached him playfully. 'I don't have to do that. The Lord knows my size.'

Laughingly they removed the coat from the wrappings and Nana put it on. It did fit. Perfectly!

Instances such as these made a deep impression upon Don's life.

On another Sunday afternoon, they had been out in the open air witnessing. On the way back a thunder storm overtook them, flooding the country roads that marked their way home.

Nana responded to the inconvenience by singing the hymn 'God leads His dear children along' at the top of her voice. 'Some through the waters, some through the flood. Some through the fire, but all through the blood,' she shrilled cheerfully, dispelling any tendency to gloom or irritation on the part of her companions.

Any time they passed a cemetery in their sorties out of town, Nana would say, 'Don, one of these days all those graves are going to open, and those that love the Lord will be caught up to be with Him. Sad to say, those who don't love the Lord will be judged. And,' she would add jauntily, 'I may be getting on in years, but I'm not looking for the undertaker. I'm looking for the Uptaker.'

It is quite a few years now since the Uptaker came to take Nana Williams to her heavenly home, but to Evangelist Don Double, her sojourn down here will always remain a fragrant memory.

8

Laying Foundations

Once Don began to preach there was no holding him. Under the designation 'Village Revivals' he started to hire halls in the villages and towns surrounding Ipswich for Saturday night rallies, as well as engaging in a good deal of open-air witness.

From the outset a small team of volunteers always accompanied Don, some of his earliest associates being his friends the Wakelings and a West Indian guitarist named George. He was also joined on occasions by a Mr and Mrs Wilce from the Elim Church.

Brother Wilce had no legs, having lost them during the war. He moved around by swinging on his arms to which two wooden platforms were attached. These he would place one in front of the other as if they were feet, dragging himself along behind.

Brother Wilce had a radiant testimony, and the object lesson, that adversity need not hinder one's usefulness for God, was not lost on Don.

Then late in the summer of 1957 Don decided to take a little day trip to Great Yarmouth. After enjoying a couple of hours on the beach it occurred to him to call on Vic Ramsay, whom he had not seen since the memorable evening in the Hadleigh Town Hall three years previously.

Vic and his wife were running a guest house at the time, although Vic himself was often away on evangelistic crusades. Happily, he happened to be at home on this occasion.

In spite of the fact that it was the busy season for hoteliers, Vic and his gracious wife Janet welcomed Don warmly.

This renewed contact resulted in an invitation to assist in Brother Ramsey's crusades, since Vic felt the Lord directing him to work in East Anglia at that time. Don gladly accepted the invitation, becoming a valuable part of the team whenever Brother Ramsey was operating in the area.

Don did not actually preach at these crusades, but booked halls, arranged advertising, put out chairs, stewarded, looked after the bookstall and sometimes led the meetings.

Still working at Kleen-Eze at this particular period, Don could take time off whenever he needed to be free for these activities. Financially it was rough, and sometimes the main meal of the day would be only bread and jam. 'But,' Don comments, 'Vic's crusades provided a fine training ground.'

At the end of one very successful campaign at Stowmarket; Brother Ramsey baptized Don's parents along with several others. There had been a marked change in Don's father for some months, but he had never said anything openly about his inner experiences. Now at his baptism he satisfied Don's curiosity by testifying, 'I accepted the Lord in my own bedroom.'

Don also followed Peter Scothern's ministry in those early years, sometimes travelling hundreds of miles at weekends to be present at his meetings. On these occasions he saw many wonderful evidences of the Lord's healing power. One particular incident he has good reason to remember.

A lady who received healing at one of Mr Scothern's London services dispensed with a huge spinal contraption (which consisted of a cage with a bar up the back that went around the neck and head) as well as leg braces and crutches.

At a subsequent meeting in Croydon, Surrey, Don had the job of carrying this paraphernalia in, so that it could be displayed while the lady gave her testimony. With the cage under one arm, and a huge bundle of calipers, crutches and what have you sticking out from under the other, he struggled down the aisle leaving a small trail behind him, much to the amusement of the gathering congregation.

Don also did quite a bit of stewarding and counselling at Peter Scothern's services, and was often there to assist when some who were prayed for fell down under the power of God.

'On more than one occasion', he recalls, 'I was also "slain" by the power,' the most significant occasion being a special ordination service at the Friends Meeting House, London, one Whit Monday afternoon. When Peter prayed for Don, he fell right over backwards and was out for quite a while.

All these experiences, both practical and spiritual, were invaluable to Don as he returned to his own local outreach in Ipswich and the surrounding district; often carrying with him a new and powerful anointing of the Spirit of God.

Gradually, as Don's ministry began to mature, invitations started to come in from a variety of churches, to take weekend evangelistic meetings, until he found himself travelling extensively.

By this time, the Ipswich Revival Fellowship, led by Mr Smith, had ceased to function as such, and Don had opened his own home for a week-night Bible study.

He had a mortgage on a semi-detached three-bedroomed house in Hazelcroft Road, and this became the scene of many remarkable happenings, conversions

46

and healings being weekly occurrences.

From the outset, numbers increased rapidly. Young and old came in from all over the area, many being contacts from Don's evangelistic outreach in the villages. One man regularly hitch-hiked sixty to seventy miles in order to be present.

A good percentage of the congregation consisted of West Indian immigrants who, streaming into Ipswich where work was available, could not seem to settle into the regular English churches. The informality of Don's house meetings being more to their liking, they flocked in, bringing their own characteristic and lively contribution to the gatherings. They would crowd into the modest house, covering every inch of available floor space, overflowing into the hallway, and up the staircase.

As the size of the Fellowship increased, meetings were held in various homes on different days, but with the main mid-week Bible study always at Hazelcroft Road, until finally they had to move into public halls to accommodate the crowds. Some of the most outstanding miracles of those days included the healing of a number of arthritic cases, as well as many deaf people.

One unforgettable healing occurred when Don prayed for a youth who had no arches in his feet. Arches appeared right there in the meeting, and the delighted young man paraded around in his hose displaying the miracle to the excited onlookers.

During this period of Don's ministry various new friends joined his team on a temporary basis. Among them were 'a very precious West Indian brother by the name of Lennox Tross' and a West Indian pastor Martin Simmonds who became a close friend and associate in the work in Ipswich, and many others.

Various musicians also joined Don from time to time,

including Arthur Tyte, a talented guitarist and singer of western-style songs. Arthur was also a member of Peter Scothern's team and in between these activities pastored a church in St Blazey, Cornwall, a town which was destined, in the purposes of God, to become a link between Don's past and his future.

Then at one of the monthly rallies sponsored by the fellowship, Don met Pop Booth. Already well into his sixties, Pop was a happy, sprightly character, with a halo of white hair and few inhibitions. He saw the piano unoccupied and making a bee-line was soon swinging the congregation along in a lively chorus.

'Billy Bray the second,' thought Don as he watched his antics, and being without a musician at the time, he invited Pop to join the team. The elderly enthusiast accepted with alacrity and during the ensuing years became a familiar figure at Don's crusades.

Pop recognized his particular gift from the Lord as being that of 'helps'. Besides being able to play and sing, and give a lengthy testimony, he always carried around with him a big bag of tools. Anything that needed mending, Pop mended it, always seeking to live up to the motto that he still has hanging on his living room wall, 'Do it, and it's done.'

Pop continued in Don's team for many years, only giving up when advancing age made the strenuous life well-nigh impossible.

Another regular activity of Don's team during the Ipswich days was to go out into the teenage cafés, and other places where young people would congregate, and seek to win them to the Lord. One evening Don and three other men started out with that intention, but found themselves instead inside a taxi office.

Don does not recall specifically what prompted them to enter, but that the leading came from God soon became evident. As they opened the door, poised for action, Gospel tracts in hand, a young man dressed in Teddy-boy gear with his back towards them, wheeled around, eyes wild and desperate-looking. In his hand he held an open pen-knife.

Don and his friend took in the situation at a glance. They had just startled a would-be suicide about to slash his wrists. In a moment they were at his side relieving him of the pen-knife and leading him to Jesus.

Meanwhile a couple of the team were soon dealing with another Teddy-boy who had entered in an ugly mood, fists raised looking for a fight. He too was broken by the power of God, dissolving into tears as he allowed the men to pray for him.

It seems the word soon went around that something unusual was happening in the taxi office, because another fellow walked right in and told the team with tears, 'I am ashamed of myself. I have been backsliding for three years.' And yet another, 'I have committed adultery. Will God forgive me for this?' The Spirit of God was moving in an almost startling way.

By now, Don's Ipswich outreach had moved into the Red Cross Hall in Berners Street, and regular Sunday services had been commenced. This work became known as the Ipswich Miracle Revival Centre, the Rev Martin Simmonds carrying much of the teaching ministry, especially when Don had to be out of town.

After Don left for full time evangelism, Mr Simmonds assumed full responsibility, and the work eventually linked up with a West Indian denomination.

In June 1961 Don put out his first copy of what in time became his quarterly magazine *Ripened Grain*. This first edition consisted of a duplicated, double-sided sheet 10 inches by 8 inches. This soon increased to six or eight duplicated pages, and by the New Year 1963 *Ripened Grain* had become a small printed magazine.

Besides Don's direct evangelistic activities, he also instituted a telephone prayer service, and a free library, the latter being cared for by a young lady originally from Jersey, known as Sister Doreen.

Don was now travelling very widely at weekends, sometimes over two hundred miles, returning late on a Sunday night ready for his salesman's rounds on Monday morning. His work with Turner's involved an early start and more driving, often about 150 miles a day. Deep down in his heart Don knew God was calling him out of secular employment into full time evangelism, and he often found himself arguing with the Lord about it.

Didn't he have a family? Didn't he have a mortgage on a house? Didn't he have commitments amounting to about £12 a week before they even began to eat, and that on a wage of less than £20? How could he give up his job?

Not that Don had not had personal experiences of the Lord's provision. On the contrary. He would recall for example the occasion when he had bought his first car. He had seen the vehicle he wanted—an old utility Ford priced £100. Since he only had £50 he offered the dealer £80 arranging to bring the money and collect the car five days later.

The appointed day arrived. He still had only £50. Undaunted, Don prepared to go out. Surely God would make a way. The Lord knew how much he needed that car. .

Within minutes a knock came at the door. Don opened it to find a man from the church standing there. His friend handed him an envelope which Don received wonderingly as if it were a missive from heaven itself. Inside lay the needed £30.

Then again, it wasn't likely he would ever forget that evening early in his Christian life when he heard the Lord telling him to put all the money he had in the offering.

It had been a Friday night and he had just been paid! What would he and the family live on during the following week? Well, if it had been merely a supersensitive conscience urging him to make the sacrifice in answer to some high-pressured appeal, he might have found himself in trouble. But no, Don recognized the quiet compelling of the Holy Spirit and obeyed with abandonment, his heart feeling as light as his pocket as he returned home.

Next morning Don had received a cheque in the post—the first ever, for more than double the amount he had put in the offering.

Yes, Don knew God could provide a table in the wilderness. Why then should he hesitate now, when God was calling him to full-time ministry? It wasn't so much that he didn't believe. Rather he felt entangled in his commitments, and in all honesty didn't know how to make the break. 'But,' says Don, 'God prepared a great fish to swallow me, just as he did for the disobedient prophet Jonah.'

Don's 'fish' was a huge, high lorry, almost as big as today's juggernauts, with a spare wheel at the back.

One Monday evening driving along the A45 coming into Ipswich on his way home from work, following a tiring weekend, Don fell asleep at the wheel. His little Austin A35 van went right underneath the massive lorry which was travelling slowly up hill just ahead of him. It hit the spare wheel and bounced back, at which moment Don woke up. Meanwhile the lorry driver went on his way completely unaware of the little drama in which he had just been involved. Don drew in to the next lay-by and inspected the damage—nothing but a dented radiator grid.

'Lord,' Don breathed, 'I got the message. I know what you're saying to me. Yes, I'll go into evangelism full time. But Lord,' he added, 'you'll have to do it. If you really want me out, then you put me out.'

'A dangerous prayer,' Don cautions, and not without reason, for within weeks his circumstances underwent a dramatic change. Heartbreaking and traumatic in their outworking, they stripped him of every weight which could have impeded his onward course and the fulfilment of his calling. At this time he entered into an experience not unlike that of Job, who lost family, friends, business and health. Concerning these events, Don has chosen to follow the injunction of Paul and 'forgetting those things which are behind', to reach out for that which is before him in the ever unfolding will of God.

9

No Turning Back

Bridges burned, Don said his last farewells to his friends at Turners and set his face towards full-time ministry and the unknown future. The manager and several other Christian employees shook his hand and assured him of their prayers.

The sceptics had their say too. One woman told him, 'You'll be out of the ministry and back in secular employment within twelve months—you mark my words.'

Don didn't. He says, 'I rejected that bad seed, and believed that the God who called me would keep me out in the centre of His will.'

But driving through the gates for the last time with his 'cards' and final wage-packet, Don felt very much alone.

'Yes, and where will next week's wages come from?' Satan seemed to be taunting.

At that moment scarcely a hundred yards from the gate, Don saw the caretaker waving him down. Don drew up and rolled down the window. 'Wait a minute,' the man called, darting into his house. He reappeared seconds later and with a 'God bless you Mr Double' pressed a £5 note into the young evangelist's hand. Don thanked him warmly, his eyes a little moist, and drove on.

'Take that, devil,' he laughed exultantly as the countryside sped by. 'I never earned £5 in three minutes before, while working in there.'

The first crusade after launching out into full-time ministry took Don and his 'Voice of Deliverance Team' of eight to Jersey, the largest of the Channel Islands, ninety miles from England and about ten miles off the coast of France.

The only preparation that had been made had been the booking of the Horticultural Hall in St Helier, the capital, and the distribution of literature by Sister Doreen and Pat Wakeling who had gone ahead earlier. The team arrived still not knowing where they would lay their heads, but eventually found lodgings of a sort.

With three days still to go to the commencement of the crusade and with hardly any funds, they were very much dependent upon the Lord to meet their needs.

Don recalls how four of them in one billet were down on their knees praying, and just wondering where their next meal would come from, when a man whom he had only met casually earlier in the day arrived at the door.

'The Lord told me to bring you this,' he smiled, handing in a big box of groceries, which included four frozen roast beef dinners.

At eight-thirty they had been praying on empty stomachs. At eight-fifty they were sitting around eating delicious roast beef. Yes, a life of faith is never dull.

The anointing of the Holy Spirit clearly rested on the crusade right from the beginning, and whether in the regular meetings or out in the open air, people responded to the call of Christ.

During the two weeks over forty people made commitments to the Lord for the first time, and several backsliders found their way back to the cross. Many with physical infirmities received healing, while others hungry for a new dimension in Christian living experienced the infilling of the Holy Spirit. The autumn edition of *Ripened Grain* in 1961 includes a number of written testimonies sent in after the team returned, telling of the varied, yet tangible blessings received, at this the team's first full-time evangelistic venture.

Shortly after the Jersey victories had passed into history, the team embarked on their next assignment, an eight-day crusade at Braintree, Essex, which proved to be a great contrast.

Except for the weekends when friends from further afield arrived to support the effort, the meetings were very poorly attended, and finances literally hit rock bottom. To cap it all, towards the end of the crusade Don's faithful friends the Wakelings, who had a little daughter to consider, felt they must return to secular employment.

Don understood, but it was a bitter blow. With his own personal griefs compounding his problems, the Braintree crusade is stamped upon his mind as 'the worst affair I ever had'.

Fighting despondency throughout the week, Don felt in no mood for the arrival of a book of poems! He had just started a bookstall, and had written to America for a number of faith-building books, particularly requesting three of each of the writings of E. W. Kenyon. The books arrived together with the bill, at the psychologically unfortunate moment when he had next to nothing to pay it with.

He looked through the literature. There were three each of *Kenyon's Living Poems*.

Don looked at the latter with something akin to disgust. Poems were just not in his line of thinking. 'Who is going to buy poems?' he asked himself. 'Who wants that kind of stuff? I'll never sell them. Yet I'm obliged to pay for them. Here I am with next to nothing, and now I've got to pay for books nobody will want.'

In his depressed state of mind, Don reacted with uncharacteristic fury and bitterness. 'Poems! Whatever next! This is it, Lord. This is the end! I'll just have to go back and get a job.'

That night after the meeting when Don went home to his temporary 'digs' he took a copy of the book of poems with him. Perhaps he subconsciously wanted to prove his point and nurse his misery a bit. Whatever his reason for doing so, he opened the book to have a look—Poems! Ugh!

He turned to the last page—his usual method of scanning a book, and his eyes fell on the very last poem:

> When I would falter or stop on the way,
> My heart lose courage, and I fail to pray,
> Remind me dear Lord, of that cross on the hill,
> Of the Man Who hung there, Love's mission
>   to fill.

Don's eyes filled with tears as he read on:

> When I am tempted to forget my call,
> Abandon my mission, forsake it all,
> Remind me dear Lord, of that cross on the hill,
> Of the Man Who hung there, Love's mission
>   to fill.
>
> When I am weary and worn by the fight,
> The way grows lonely and dark is the night,
> Remind me dear Lord, of that cross on the hill,
> Of the Man Who hung there, Love's mission
>   to fill. . . .

Don dropped to his knees and wept. There and then he repented of his failure to embrace the cross, and of his near decision to turn aside from his calling.

Renewing his vows and accepting God's forgiveness, Don found again the peace that passes all understanding. 'That was seventeen or more years ago,' he muses, 'and I've never looked back since.'

One Sunday morning not long after this, as Don lay on his bed waiting on the Lord in prayer, God gave him a vision. We use the word advisedly in a day when the expression is often applied very loosely.

Don saw himself preaching in a sandy, dusty park compound area. The vast congregation included people of all colours; negroid, caucasian and mongoloid types.

He had no idea what the vision could mean, but simply held it in his heart for future reference.

Thirteen years later in his Dar Es Salaam Crusade, Tanzania, November 1974, Don saw the vision fulfilled to the last detail.

As he stood in the great enclosure preaching to nearly 15,000 people—Africans, Indians, Chinese, Europeans—everything, even to the wooden platform and the fence which consisted of nothing but poles joined together with string, corresponded exactly with what he had seen on that distant Sunday morning as he lay upon his bed.

Why did God give Don that glimpse into the future so many years ahead of the event? Don answers, 'I believe it was to keep me with a vision. I would never have envisaged going to Africa, or flying around the world in those days, for I was very much a home bird.'

Encouraged by this experience, Don now sought the Lord for the next step. Unexpectedly, the Spirit moved upon him to make a 750-mile trip to Cornwall, where all unknown to the young evangelist a whole new sphere of ministry and adventure awaited him.

10

Heather

Don set out alone on his long trip to Cornwall, hardly knowing what to expect on arrival but with a strong sense of the Lord's hand upon him. En route he called to see some close friends, Pastor and Mrs Downs of the Assemblies of God.

This godly couple had a great influence on Don during the early days of full-time ministry and in many respects were like another 'mum and dad' to him. Concerning Pastor Downs Don says, 'I never met another man who fulfilled the role of a pastor as well as he did. In fact Pastor Downs himself believed God had given him a specialist ministry to what he called "broken-wing Christians".'

Don ate with relish the hearty breakfast Mrs Downs set before him, for it was still early. After a brief time of fellowship, his resources replenished, he continued his journey.

As he cruised along in the team's new Austin J4 van (bought with a bank loan which the Lord had quickly enabled him to pay off) the rolling countryside of the western counties seemed breathtakingly beautiful in the autumn sunshine.

Stopping here and there along the way, Don handed out tracts in villages and towns in Dorset, Devon and finally Cornwall, enjoying every moment of the journey.

Arriving in the small town of St Blazey in the late

afternoon, he took out his notebook and checked on the only address he had—that of his friend and occasional team-member, Arthur Tyte. Arthur lived in a caravan on the property of a family by the name of Martin, and pastored the small St Blazey Elim Church of which Mr Martin was the Secretary.

Believing God had directed his visit, Don made his way to the Martin's residence, fully expecting to find his friend at home. But the caravan appeared to be locked. Could Arthur be away? Don rang the Martin's door bell.

An alert, refined-looking man answered his ring and listened with interest as Don introduced himself. Then throwing wide the door invitingly, he motioned Don inside.

'Yes, the pastor is away,' Jack Martin confirmed. 'But the Lord has obviously sent you here to take our meeting tonight,' he added with enthusiasm.

Cheerful sounds and aromas wafted down the hall as Don stepped gratefully inside. One of his first impressions of the household centred around 'a whopping great blue deep-freeze in the kitchen', the first he had ever seen used by a private family.

But other impressions followed quickly. For there was nothing frozen about the Martin family or their welcome.

Mrs Martin, an outgoing lady in middle life, soon made her visitor feel at home, and they were shortly joined by the family's pretty, brown-eyed teenage daughter Heather, and Brian, her twenty year old brother. Seated together round the meal table in simple fellowship, the dedication of the whole family and their undivided concern for the things of the Lord impressed Don deeply.

An hour or so later he found himself preaching at the midweek service in the little pioneer church.

The meeting though not large, soon came alive with the presence of the Lord, and for seventeen-year old Heather held a special significance.

As Don spoke on the theme, 'If ye love me, keep my commandments,' Heather heard the voice of the Holy Spirit confirming her own call to full-time service.

Back in August she had sensed the Lord calling her out of secular employment, and had discussed with a family friend, a Methodist local preacher Edgar Trout, the possibility of becoming his secretary. Now as God reaffirmed His call on this Wednesday evening in October, she knew the time had come to act.

Next day, with the enthusiasm of youth, Heather handed in her notice to the Estate Agent's office where she worked, and that evening phoned Edgar Trout.

Don, praying in his room next to the hall where Heather was talking animatedly into the phone, could not help but overhear. As he listened, the Holy Spirit unexpectedly dropped a word into his heart, 'Heather will be your secretary.'

Meanwhile, Edgar Trout was telling Heather on the phone, 'I'll pray about it.' And there the matter rested for the time being.

By Friday, Arthur Tyte arrived back, and Don stayed on over the weekend taking part in open-air witness, a film rally at the St Blazey Labour Hall, and preaching at the Sunday services of the Elim Church.

Exciting things happened that weekend. A number of newcomers were saved and several healings took place, including a growth which disappeared right before the astonished eyes of the onlookers.

Don returned to Ipswich via Bristol, and about a week later sent Arthur Tyte an urgent letter. Out of his team of eight, only two could continue with him in the work. He had no one except elderly Pop and Lily Booth to help with the Bury St Edmunds Crusade, scheduled to commence on October 28th.

Without hesitation Arthur and his wife Joy decided to join Don for the crusade. Heather, now out of a job and awaiting the Lord's guidance, said, 'I'm doing nothing. I'll go with you.'

Mr Martin turned to his wife. 'Rhoda, you haven't had a holiday. Why don't you go along too?' Rhoda Martin may have had some doubts about the holiday aspect of the suggestion, but always happy to be actively involved in evangelism, she readily responded.

A day or two later Don greeted his new team with thankfulness and relief, while Lilian Double gamely managed to accommodate them all overnight.

Don's parents had been coping with his correspondence for him until this time, but with a trained secretary now under his roof for a few hours, Don naturally asked Heather to take a few letters. She was busily engaged in typing that evening when postman George Double walked in. After introductions and handshakes all round, Don's father looked across at Heather and said with a twinkle, 'She'll have to stay and be Don's secretary, and relieve us of a job.' Everyone laughed and made appropriate comments, but Heather just smiled and replied archly, 'No, I've already got myself a job, thank you.'

The Bury St Edmunds crusade proved to be a good one, with converts added to the local church and several outstanding healings. When the meetings ended, Don asked Heather hopefully, 'What are you doing next? I've a stack of mail. Will you stay and do some for me?'

'All right,' Heather condescended cheerfully, her mind still following a different track from Don's, 'but only until I hear from Edgar Trout.'

The days passed by. Heather dealt with the mail and prepared an issue of *Ripened Grain*. Finally, six weeks later, Mr Trout's letter arrived. Opening it eagerly,

Heather swiftly scanned the contents. '. . . .The Lord has shown me that you are not to join our "All For Christ Team" but that He has a similar ministry for you in another team,' she read.

Mildly taken aback, Heather silently handed the letter to Don, who noted the contents, nodded sympathetically, but showed no surprise. Needless to say it didn't take anyone any deep heart searchings to decide where, or what the other team referred to might be. So Heather stayed on.

Besides her secretarial duties Heather looked after the bookstall at the crusades and soon began to minister in counselling as well. 'I was thrown in at the deep end,' she recalls. 'One night I had to counsel seventy-five young people together. I'll never forget it. I literally shook in my shoes.'

But resting in the Lord, Heather found that she could cope, and soon became, together with her mother, a well-nigh indispensable part of Don's team. Thus began a partnership which in a few short years would ripen into something very precious.

But many eventful experiences lay between that winter of 1961 and a certain day as yet unforeseen in May 1964.

11

Apostle to the Villages

Don's regular team now consisted of Pop and Lily
Booth, Heather and himself, with help on occasions
from Heather's mother, and various other friends as
circumstances permitted.

The usual procedure consisted of seeking the Lord as
to the next place of ministry. Then they would contact
local clergy inviting their co-operation, distribute handbills and begin door-knocking. Follow-up was fairly
simple, the co-operating churches reaping the benefits.

Between crusades, Don would return to his parents'
home in Hadleigh, and to the Ipswich ministry where
God continued to pour out His blessing.

The first crusade of 1962 in Haverhill, West Suffolk,
stands out in the evangelist's memory as an occasion
when the Lord protected him in a unique way.

It was market day in the small country town, and the
main streets were thronged with people. The team
spent the morning door-knocking, giving out tracts on
the streets, and inviting people to the meetings.

Now on their way back for lunch Heather and her
mother, together with Don, decided to stop and buy
some floral decorations for the town hall. Heather and
Rhoda entered a green-grocer's shop where a few winter blossoms were on sale. Don stood outside gazing
through the window at the display of fruit and vegetables. An icy wind ruffled his hair and made him brace

his shoulders. 'I hope they don't take too long,' he thought to himself.

At that moment a customer started to leave the shop pushing open the door and leaving it to swing back into place. Suddenly, without warning, a gust of wind caught the door as it swung back blowing it shut with a force that shattered the large plate glass window directly in front of Don, scattering lethal pieces in all directions.

But strange to relate, Don found himself no longer there. In a split second God had transported him to the opposite side of the road, where he now stood looking on with surprise at the confusion, as the startled occupants of the shop rushed outside to better view the damage. Awed, but thankful, Don and his companions completed their purchases and continued on their way.

Haverhill was also a place where needs were met in unexpected ways. Don had booked the town hall but didn't yet have enough money to pay for it. As he went to collect the keys he wondered nervously what he should say, since the contract included payment in advance. He entered the office.

A friendly clerk looked up from his desk with a smile. 'Hello, Mr Double,' he began before Don had a chance to open his mouth. 'We have decided that as you're having the hall for two weeks you can pay at the end.' Another crisis past!

There was little money in hand for personal supplies for the team, but they would often arrive back at Don and Pop Booth's lodgings where they had the use of the kitchen, to find parcels of groceries and vegetables on the door step and oven-ready chickens and other things hanging on the door-knob. The identity of their kind benefactor remains a mystery to this day.

The crusade itself proved to be most encouraging. A nearby Assembly Church decided to support the effort, closing down their own week-night meetings in order to do so.

Naturally this faithful and enthusiastic church had the privilege of following up the hundred or so decisions, mostly among young people and children, recorded during the crusade.

Several memorable healings also took place during the week. The seventy-four-year-old pastor, the Rev. H. C. Graves, who had worn a hearing aid for thirteen years, suddenly found his hearing restored while watching a miracle film at one of the meetings.

A little cross-eyed girl of about six years, who had come to one of the services with an older brother, came out for prayer of her own accord and received an instant miracle.

Next evening she was back, and at the invitation for those with needs to step forward she came out again. Don bent down low. 'And what do you want tonight dear?' he queried kindly. The little child looked up happily. 'I've just come back to say "thank you" to Jesus,' she responded, setting off a murmur of rejoicing and praise throughout the congregation.

In some places where Don crusaded, the meetings were given front page coverage in the press, and opportunities occurred at times to speak over local radio stations.

Something of the young evangelist's zeal will be felt in this quote from his 1962 summer issue of *Ripened Grain:*

Since our last issue our ministry has increased on every hand . . . hundreds of souls have confessed their new-found faith in Christ, miracles of healing have been the talk of the locality as curved spines have straightened, cancers withered and deaf ears opened. Many have been revived and our water baptismal services have been a stirring feature in all our crusades. The press has given unbiased reports which have been glorifying to the God we serve, and not to man. Hallelujah!

Ranging from north to south, Don continually sought to fulfil the call to preach the Gospel in the small towns and villages, and has often been referred to as 'an apostle to the villages'.

In 1963 he wrote, 'I confess that many times I have been tempted to hold crusades in larger towns and cities because of the easiness of getting a crowd together, but to God be the glory, His grace has been sufficient. God allows me to take rallies or weekends in the bigger places, but not crusades. Jesus in His earthly ministry never neglected the villages. . . .'

Following Don's original leading to the West Country in 1961, the Holy Spirit now began to give Don a specific burden for the whole county of Cornwall, where in addition to much dead and formal religion, sun-worship was in vogue and witchcraft rampant. 'Cornwall is less evangelized than Nigeria,' an evangelist just returned from Calabar told him. Consequently, Don began to concentrate more of his efforts on that part of the country, eventually setting up his headquarters there.

It was while on the way to a crusade in Lothwithiel, Cornwall, in June 1962 that Don, together with Heather and team member Evangelist Tony Holloway, experienced another miracle of God's protective power.

Passing through Saltash, they were cruising along at about thirty-five miles per hour, when a parked post-office van on the opposite side of the road took off without warning. Apparently unconscious of their presence, it drove right across their path.

Don slammed on the brakes in a vain attempt to avoid the inevitable crash. At the moment of impact, as if rehearsed for the act, Don, Heather and Tony, all sitting together at the front, in the one and only seat, shouted 'Jesus' at the tops of their voices.

Their vehicle hit the post-office van broadside on, knocking it over on its side, where it hit the ground and bounced up again. The controls around Don's feet were twisted, but apart from a bruised arm, he and his companions were unharmed.

Police soon arrived at the scene and the postal employee went off to hospital with a slight cut on his head. One officer remarked to Don afterwards that he didn't know how he and his party had escaped injury, which provided Don the perfect cue to tell him, 'Well, the Bible says, "Whosoever shall call on the name of the Lord shall be saved." We called, and the Lord saved us.'

In October of 1962 the team descended on Cornwall again, crusading in town after town over a period of several months.

The Polperro crusade proved to be the most outstanding during this period. An attractive fishing village with a population of under two thousand, Polperro didn't appear at first to be destined for a successful campaign. To start with Don had great difficulty in getting a meeting place.

He wrote to the owners of the Free Forresters Hall asking for its use. They said no. He wrote again, 'Please reconsider.' They answered in the negative. Sure of his guidance Don could not take no for an answer. He wrote again, 'God wants us to have that hall.' Victory at last! They consented.

The first night drew a poor attendance, but the support of a group of middle-aged Methodists encouraged the team. These good folk had been saved in their youth during a visitation of the Holy Spirit, and had kept up a Saturday night prayer meeting for twenty-five years. Praying in recent years especially for the younger generation, many of whom were far from the Lord, they were now about to see the answer to those prayers.

The weather that January, 1963, was reported by the locals as 'the worst in living memory'. The hall itself proved to be far from inviting, being difficult to heat and with ice often forming on the insides of the windows. Yet in spite of these hindrances, as prayer began to prevail the people came, and the meeting scheduled for ten days had to be continued for six weeks.

Many of the people walking to the crusade wore socks over their boots to prevent them slipping on the ice. Some brought along hot-water bottles and blankets for their comfort, and the hall would fill up a good hour before the meetings were due to begin.

Dozens of people including whole families found the Lord. Ten were baptized in water, and many received the baptism in the Holy Spirit. Wonderful miracles of healing took place every night. '. . . Cripples walked, the dumb spoke, and those with eye afflictions were healed. . . .'

A tremendous spirit of intercession seemed to pervade the meetings. Prayer just flowed. Don says, 'I literally had to stop them praying in order to start preaching. It was the nearest thing to a revival I have ever seen in this country.'

In such an atmosphere the gifts of the Spirit manifested with great freedom. At one meeting the 'gift of faith' came upon Don. He stood up and proclaimed in the Spirit, 'I guarantee that every sick person here tonight who comes forward will be healed.' Don listened to himself in amazement, wondering at his own audacity. But God was in it and did not fail him. People with all kinds of infirmities came out, some on sticks and crutches, and God healed them all.

On another evening during the same crusade, after the last enquirer had been counselled and sent home, the team went out into the bitter cold night to find themselves locked out of their van. The keys had been left inside!

What should they do? Where could they get help at this late hour? To add to the sense of urgency, Evangelist Harry Greenwood and his wife Pam, who were part of the team on this occasion, had a young baby at home waiting for its night feed.

'Let's pray,' Pam urged.

As the group bowed their heads in prayer and committed their situation to the Lord, Don felt again that quickening of audacious faith, as the Holy Spirit whispered, 'Go and open the door.'

Don strode over to the van and the door opened to his touch. But the lock was still engaged and Don had to take the keys out of the ignition to unlock it, before he could shut the door from the inside.

Commenting on these remarkable happenings Don says, 'In those days we were very new in this realm of the Spirit and being new we were fearless to speak whatever God told us.'

The follow-up of the Polperro Crusade was left in the hands of Harry Greenwood, with whom Don had recently become acquainted. Harry became a very close friend and associate, often sharing with Don in the ministry in between his own evangelistic activities. Just how close the sense of oneness in the Spirit became is best illustrated by a strange and amusing incident.

There had been no news of Harry for a couple of weeks, although they were expecting him to join them for a crusade. Unknown to the team, Harry was passing through a difficult time financially. Having neither money for petrol or even a stamp for a letter, he was just waiting on the Lord for His supply.

Meanwhile, Don's van began to act very strangely. Whereas it usually did a mileage of about twenty-five miles to the gallon, it began to do a low fifteen miles per gallon. This continued over a period of ten days or so.

Eventually, Harry turned up in his bone-shaker of a car, described as being 'literally held together with bits of wire and pieces of string'. He announced that he had driven nearly a hundred miles on one gallon of petrol!

But where had Don's fuel been disappearing to? After Harry's arrival, mysteriously, Don's van began to function normally again.

Could it have been merely coincidence? Angelic involvement? Who dares say? The reader will no doubt make his own assessment on the basis of his knowledge of the ways and power of God.

Early in 1964 Don returned to Cornwall again for concentrated crusades, and then again in October 1965 for his Major Cornwall Crusade, which covered a period of six months. They booked the largest halls in faith, and contacted local churches. Many denominations came in and supported the work, which resulted in unusual unity and blessing. In Launceston in particular they experienced a real visitation of the Spirit.

Between ten-day crusades in each major area they held film rallies in various towns, including a monthly rally in Par. Regular rallies also commenced in Callington Town Hall with chairs filling the aisles to accommodate the overflow.

Saltash and Mevagissey were other places which felt a touch of revival. In meetings packed to the doors many found salvation and wholeness in Christ. Cornwall, the county known as 'the evangelists' graveyard', was experiencing a resurrection.

During those early days in Cornwall, the Lord gave Don a new name for his crusades which until then had been known as 'Miracle Crusades'.

The change came about on the advice of a dear old Methodist local preacher. A man of character and power whom even the unbelievers in the village respected, Reg Warne could remember the days when conviction of the Spirit was so strong that men would jump over the formes to get to the communion rail to be saved.

This old gentleman came to see Don one day and offered some fatherly advice which Don declares became a turning point in his ministry.

'Don,' the old man counselled, 'to advertise healing as the major thrust of your ministry is not good. It puts people off whom you could otherwise help. And not only that, but people who might help you—won't. I suggest you get some other name.'

Don pondered the question for a while and together with his team prayed it over. Shortly afterwards the Lord gave them the new name 'Good News Crusade'.

About this time, with increasing amounts of finance flowing through the accounts, income tax began to be a problem. Accordingly in 1965 they decided to become a registered religious charity, with Tony Holloway, Rhoda Martin, George Double, and Don and Heather as the trustees.

From that time onwards, the Good News Crusade continued to grow in influence and blessing, reaching out like a benevolent giant octopus in its many facets of ministry.

12

'Many Irons...'

From the first days of his public ministry, Don has always had a varied and prodigious number of undertakings on hand.

Early copies of *Ripened Grain* advertise a free lending library which in the days of cheaper postage was quite well used. 'We still have the library today,' says Don, 'but our main aim now is to have books available that are of real value, although out of print.'

Then there was the 'book room' which, starting off as a corner in Don's mother's home, was later relocated in St Austell and has grown into a sizable and well stocked store. Two more bookshops have since been added to the crusade's activities, one in Hereford and the other in Exmouth.

Ripened Grain also mentions in those early days a 'telephone prayer service' manned by 'whoever happened to be at home'. Urgent prayer requests were sent on to Don as quickly as possible. 'This ministry is still available,' he says, 'although we don't actually advertise it as such. People phone and we remember any such requests at our Monday night team prayer meeting.'

When questioned about the practice of sending to the sick handkerchiefs that have been prayed over, Don replies, 'The ministry of prayer cloths is something we did use at one time . . . but as my ministry matured I became less happy about it and would not advertise this kind of service now. However, we do still on occasion, when specifically directed by the Holy Spirit, pray over a cloth and send it to a sick person who has written in for prayer.'

Don also made good use of Gospel films in his early crusades, often holding 'film rallies'. In more recent years he has not used these visual aids in his actual crusade meetings, but a film unit was still available as a separate ministry for many years, mainly taken care of by one of his younger team members. It has now been sent to the mission field in Tanzania.

Parcels of free tracts were also available to anyone on request. In 1963 *Ripened Grain* announced the Two Million Tract Crusade, when supporters were urged to use the literature widely to help get out the Gospel. Don, the man who formerly could not read or write adequately, even wrote a tract *That Certain Void* with Heather's help.

As early as 1961 *Ripened Grain* urged readers to 'send a gift for one of our limited number of tape recordings, on a fourteen days' loan'. Several years later a full scale 'Good News Crusade Tape Library' came into being, with 'hundreds of faith inspiring messages' available on a free-will-offering basis. Hundreds now are sold after each major GNC event.

Free literature was also sent overseas as requests came in from Nigeria and other places. This included brand new Bibles, New Testaments and Gospel Portions. Also, 'second hand clothing to send to those in need'. These departments operated from Mrs Martin's home in St Blazey Gate, Par.

In later years bicycles, a car, a motor cycle, two Land Rovers, Gospel tents and other equipment—not to mention thousands of pounds sterling—have been sent out to various mission fields by the Good News Crusade.

And GNC is constantly providing such equipment to the mission fields where God has given them an involvement. These projects are usually promoted at the popular Easter Convention.

Another such project involved the purchase of five thousand Bibles which have been put into Kenya prisons.

The Easter Convention started in a small way as part of a crusade which extended over the Easter period at Southwold, Suffolk in 1959. By 1962 the convention moved to the Scout Hall in Ipswich where it became an annual event for many years. In 1975, to accommodate the increasing number of visitors, it moved to the Garret Memorial Hall, Ipswich; and in 1976 to the United Reformed Church in Tacket Street, Ipswich. And now it may move again, this time to Norwich.

During the early years the Hungarian evangelist, Don Oldon, took a leading part. Gradually other well-known names came to be associated with the convention, including the Rev. David Greenow, Judson Cornwall, Bob Buess, Don Gossett, Arthur Wallis, Bryn Jones, and countless others.

One year, an American evangelist by the name of the Rev. Drummond Thom turned up. Somehow a copy of Don's magazine had come into his hands in the States, and as he read the advertisement concerning the convention in Ipswich, God spoke to him, telling him to take a plane immediately and go.

He set out to New York in faith, preached in a Baptist Church where they took up a 'love offering' for him, and bought a one-way ticket to England. He arrived at the Easter Convention and introduced himself. Don looked at the new arrival cautiously. You can't invite every Tom, Dick and Harry on to your platform without knowing something about them. But Drummond Thom gave a good impression and Don let him give a short word. 'His ministry was so blessed,' says Don, 'that we put him on again and used him, and he became a great personal friend. He has been back several times since.'

Many wonderful things happened at the Easter Convention. A Salvation Army Captain by the name of Brian Eastwell was one of many who received a mighty outpouring of the Spirit of God there. He later joined the team for a while in the capacity of Crusade Manager.

Numerous healings have taken place over the years, one of the most outstanding being the case of seventy-one-year-old Mrs Alice Wade. Her testimony appeared in the 1964 New Year Issue of *Ripened Grain*. Suffering from cancer, an enlarged kidney, a diseased liver and a crumbling spine, she had endured six operations and had been given up to die. Her pastor, the Rev. R. Sherrington of the Chelmsford Free Church, managed to get her to the Easter Convention of the Good News Crusade.

'I was in intense pain and do not know how I sat through the afternoon service,' she wrote afterwards. '. . .At the end of the evening service I went forward into the prayer line with many others to have hands laid on me in the name of the Lord Jesus Christ. The moment this happened, the power of God went right through me like an electric shock. At that moment all the intense pain I had known for so long left my body.

'I went home and after that day never took another tablet and had no more injections . . . I no longer wear my spinal support . . . I now mow my own lawn and dig my own garden . . . the neighbours are all shocked at what God has done for me. . . .'

This testimony is typical of what God is continuing to do year by year in the Easter Convention. And yet every year is different, for as Don never tires of emphasizing, 'the Holy Spirit is original. No two services should ever be exactly alike.'

At the Easter Convention, as in all of Don Double's meetings, there is joy and freedom and a spirit of praise, which break down barriers of formality and tradition.

Naturally, a few find the meetings a bit too lively, especially at the beginning, but most who stay on get caught up in the blessing, and by the last night may even find themselves literally dancing with joy along with the rest.

It is not surprising that even back in the early years Don Oldon delighted in referring to the Easter gathering as 'An Unconventional Convention'.

13

Itinerating

May 9th, 1964, holds a special place in the records of the Good News Crusade, for on that day, Don and Heather were joined together in marriage at the Leek Seed Methodist Church, St Blazey Gate, in the presence of ninety guests, many of them fellow ministers of the Gospel.

At the reception following, held in the Sunday School Hall beside the church, Evangelist David Greenow read out six stanzas of a poem which had come to him in the Spirit that morning—the first time, he said, that he had ever received poetry from the Lord.

Pastor Bert England related how during the service he had seen in vision a couple walking along a narrow pathway through a stormy sea—one very tall, the other not so tall. He said it was obvious who they were—Don and Heather. Then he added in the spirit of prophecy, 'If these two keep right on in the centre of the path, in the centre of the will of God, the storms and the waves will come, but nothing will be able to touch them or their marriage.'

In this unusual way God confirmed His blessing upon the union, and many of the guests afterwards referred to the whole occasion as 'a wonderful spiritual experience'.

The happy couple left for a short honeymoon in the Scilly Isles off the coast of Cornwall. But even there they could not resist slipping a Gospel tract in as many doors as possible on the islands they visited during the five days.

They returned from their honeymoon rejoicing in the Lord's goodness, and continued their busy but exciting ministry.

For the first few years after their marriage, Don and Heather lived mainly out of suitcases, itinerating from crusade to crusade and lodging in a variety of places.

Once, when invited to conduct meetings in Thetford, they arrived to find the only accommodation provided for the whole team consisted of one room about ten feet square.

Don and the men slept in this room while Heather had no option but to make her bed in the van outside. But they cheerfully accepted the bad with the good and occasionally even had the luxury of a caravan to themselves.

Between crusades they would make their way to Hadleigh where Don's parents cared for the children, now at school, or to St Blazey where they boarded with the Martins.

Many a time they would find themselves reduced to almost their last penny, but God never let them down. On one occasion a pound note arrived all the way from Nigeria, and saved them from a hungry day.

Another time when Don was in Northamptonshire and short of money, he drove into a garage in faith that God would supply his need of petrol.

'Fill her up,' he told the attendant boldly. At that moment he looked up, and who should be walking across the petrol-station yard, but an acquaintance who lived three hundred miles away?

Delighted to see Don, the friend came across and chatted for a few moments. Then turning to the attendant who by now had completed the filling operation, he took out his wallet saying, 'I'll pay for this,' and Don drove off, thrilled again at the timeliness of his Father's provision.

But while God's supply was an ever present reality, Satan's opposition could be very real too.

In 1966, three months before the birth of their son Stephen, Don and Heather went to the Royal Albert Hall to hear the Rev. David Wilkerson and left their beautiful new car in Hyde Park. When they returned several hours later—shock! The car had disappeared, and with it practically everything they personally owned.

Not having a home of their own, Don and Heather carried most of their few possessions with them. These included (in addition to clothing) typewriters, camera, a leather case, and other personal effects. Also a silver bracelet given to Heather when she was twelve years old by her dying grandmother—made from a family heirloom; and a silver locket, Don's first gift to her. Most disturbing of all, apart from the car itself, a lovely outfit for the new baby had also gone; it had been purchased only two days previously with money provided specifically for the purpose.

Don and Heather and team member the Rev. John McLauchlan eyed one another in dismay. 'Brother John,' Don breathed, 'pray.' Then as Mr McLauchlan began to lift his voice to God in prayer, Don and Heather joined in softly.

Praising God together the sense of shock soon passed and they were filled with peace. 'Thank you, Jesus. Praise the Lord,' they responded, adding this one petition: 'But please, Lord, do let us find the car. And don't let the thief take our Bibles.'

They made their way out of the darkened park to the railway station and took a train to Hackney where they were due to stay the night with friends. Next day, they bought a set of underwear each, and an extra shirt for Don, and set off in a borrowed car to fulfil commitments in Bournemouth.

Three weeks later the police traced the stolen vehicle abandoned in a car park, six miles from where it had been taken. In it they found a pair of Don's shoes, which the thief had apparently decided were too large for his use, and the Bibles.

The Lord brought them through these trials and gradually restored everything needful, even providing two sets of baby clothes, a double supply of nappies, and two carry-cots, which led them to wonder if twins were imminent. Instead, they met a Christian couple who had just welcomed an addition to the family, and had next to nothing for the child. Gladly they shared with them the Lord's bounty.

Meanwhile, although Don's ministry took him far and wide, his specific burden for the West Country caused him to turn his thoughts more and more to Cornwall as the place for setting up a permanent headquarters.

His new secretary, Susan Love, handled most of the work from their temporary office—the Martins' caravan. But it was obvious that something larger would soon be needed.

A friend mentioned some rooms available over a tailor opposite Woolworths in the centre of St Austell's high street. Feeling the time had come for a step of faith, Don began negotiations, and leased the whole of the second floor. This gave them space for two offices and their first 'Good News Bookroom'.

Possessing only two suitcase-loads of books, the stocking of the shop also constituted a venture of faith. But by January 1967, with Sheila Balmforth installed as manageress, the shop had begun to function, and is now a well-stocked Christian bookshop.

Another development during this period concerned the small St Blazey church where Don had first met the Martin family. Owing to the fact that no permanent pastor could be found to shepherd the group, they had all left the Elim movement, and now met in Jack and Rhoda's home—also holding monthly rallies in a public hall. Whenever Don was in the district, he ministered and gave some oversight to the work which began to grow rapidly.

In 1965 they purchased an old Methodist Church (formerly a Bible Christian Billy Bray Chapel) and in January 1966 announced the formal opening of 'The Cornwall Evangelistic Centre'.

The centre also became the home of an annual Whitsun Conference which continued until 1971, 'at which time,' says Don, 'we felt the Lord telling us that the Whit. Conferences had fulfilled His purpose, and to discontinue them.'

In this connection Don has a strong conviction that Christians need to be sensitive to the mind of the Lord, not only in initiating new things, but also in terminating them when He has finished with their usefulness, 'lest they become nothing more than monuments to what God has done in the past, rather than a current vision of what He is doing today.'

In due time the Lord directed Don to appoint elders in the church, and Don stepped down from the leadership, becoming instead just one member of a plural oversight.

The Cornwall Evangelistic Centre, now known as Par Gospel Church, is presently rebuilding its premises. It is a fellowship that stands behind Don in all his evangelistic endeavours: always sending him and his team off with a commissioning service and the laying on of hands, whenever his crusades take him overseas.

14

Three Deliverances

There is a tendency to view with awe the man successful in his calling, and to assume that he personally has
no inner struggles or self-doubts. Such is often far from
the truth.

Don, the big rugged evangelist, preaching positive,
faith-building sermons, winning the lost and healing
the sick, at times felt very small and insignificant.

How glad he is that just as he has ministered to thousands of men and women with needs across the years,
so other members of the body of Christ under the
direction of the Holy Spirit, have ministered back to
him.

Apart from the healing ministry, Don has on three
separate occasions experienced deliverance from different aspects of spiritual bondage, through the laying
on of hands and prayer.

'To be accurate,' Don says, 'from the time of my conversion over a period of ten years or more, I was being
set free from fears which had built up during my pre-
conversion days.'

The three deliverances represent high-points in this
process, and all occurred at the Charismatic Conferences
started by the late Edgar Trout at Torbay Court Hotel,
Paignton, Devon. These yearly conferences, some of the
first of their kind to be held in Britain, presented a
unique ministry in which Edgar and his team were

prominent. Since Edward's death they have been taken over by the GNC and the conference is now known as the Annual Autumn Conference.

Concerning Edgar Trout (who although having a nationwide ministry was also a Methodist local preacher, a town councillor and private business man) Don gives the following testimony.

'Edgar Trout was used of God to bless me in my ministry, more than any other man has been. He was one who lived very close to the Lord, and I held him in high esteem. If you ever went to visit him you would examine your heart, making sure you were right with God, because if not, he would very soon have a "word of knowledge" from the Lord revealing your condition.

'He was a tremendous man of faith and expected God to do great things. One of his strongest points was guidance, and one can only describe the things that happened as—amazing.'

The first Torbay Court Conference that Don attended in 1964 lasted two weeks. But Don and Heather only planned to stay one week as that was all they could afford.

At the end of the week they felt reluctant to return home, and asked the Lord if they might stay the second week. If so, please to supply the wherewithal. Within twenty-four hours an envelope containing enough money for the second week appeared anonymously under the bedroom door.

This they received thankfully, but then proceeded to ask the Lord for another sign if He really wanted them to stay.

That evening in the meeting, one of Edgar's team saw a vision of a fleece stretched out between two poles. Edgar gave the interpretation. 'There is someone here who is asking God for a sign which He has already provided. This is wrong. Accept the first sign.'

Don looked up meekly, 'That's me,' he said.

He explained the situation, whereupon Edgar replied, 'I can assure you brother, God wants you here next week.' It was during this second week that Don experienced the first of his three deliverances.

As a teenager, Don had been sitting on the beach at Clacton when a gipsy came by and offered to tell his fortune. He gave her his palm, half amused, half interested.

Now as he listened to teaching on the subject of occult bondage and the dangers of fortune-telling, horoscopes and the like, he leaned forward intently. What was that the preacher was saying?

'Many of the problems and hang-ups you experience even after conversion can be traced directly to occult bondage. If you have at some time in your life dabbled in these things, there is an area in your life where Satan still has a stake. You need deliverance from this baneful influence.

'At the close of this meeting we will pray for those who feel a need in this area. Renounce once and for all every contact with occult practices, past and present, and the Lord will set you gloriously free.'

As Don pondered these words, his first reaction was 'Well, that's ridiculous. All that was surely taken care of at conversion.'

But as he conjured up the face of the gypsy, and re-called her cajoling tones, he seemed to hear the hiss of the serpent.

'Well, I'm a reasonable kind of chap,' he said to himself. 'If there is anything in this deliverance business, I may as well find out. It won't do any harm to have them pray for me.' So Don went out.

Edgar Trout laid his hands on Don and prayed, by faith, breaking the power of occult oppression on the authority of the Word of God, and by the blood of Christ.

'Immediately,' Don says, 'I felt a wonderful sense of

release and victory.' Memories of the fortune-teller's predictions, that had bothered him at times, completely disappeared. Even more significant—he began to experience a new freedom in the ability to read and receive life from the Word of God.

The following year found Don and Heather once more at the Torbay Conference, only this time Don had been invited as one of the speakers. Again the Lord had something special in store for him.

One evening, the teaching having ended, Edgar's team moved among the congregation, praying for those with specific needs. Suddenly, Edgar Trout spoke out as he often did, 'I have a tremendous anointing for somebody.'

Feeling deeply in need of a new touch from God, Don prayed, 'Lord, send him to me.'

Mr Trout walked over to Don, 'Brother Don, I don't understand this, but the Lord says it is for you.'

'That's just what I prayed, brother,' Don answered.

Edgar laid his hands on Don's head. 'The Lord shows me there is an inferiority complex spirit which has been bothering you because of your past life. Is that true?'

'Now I was on the spot,' Don says. 'I had never heard of an inferiority complex spirit, but I certainly did have a huge inferiority complex.'

Although Don had preached and ministered among his own associates for a number of years, yet because of his lack of schooling, and a general sense of inadequacy, he often held back in the company of other ministers of repute, content to sit in a corner out of sight.

He looked up at Edgar, 'Yes, brother,' Don replied, 'it's true.' So Edgar prayed, rebuking the spirit of inferiority and casting it out in the name of Jesus.

Don says, 'Such a change took place in me that I could not recognize myself. It doesn't matter now who is around. If I were on the same platform with Billy Graham it would make no difference; because I've come to realize that the Holy Spirit in me is as good as the Holy Spirit in anyone else.'

Only once since then, and that many years later, did Don face again briefly the spectre of inferiority complex. 'I was due to speak at a certain meeting,' Don recounts. 'Four days beforehand I contacted the leader, who informed me that another brother with an outstanding ministry, whom I had not seen for fourteen years, would be present.

'Caught off guard, that old sense of inferiority hit me. Next evening, I phoned Heather and told her about it. Praise the Lord, she gave me no sympathy, but challenged me as to whether or not I was complete in Christ. I confessed that I was, and immediately felt ninety-five per cent better.

'At the meeting several days later, the other minister arrived late, by which time the room was packed, and he barely managed to squeeze inside the door. We could not even so much as greet one another.

'When the time came that I was introduced to speak, this minister began to phrophesy, ''This is my servant, whom I have sent here tonight. I shall put my word in his mouth, and because it will be my word that is spoken, take heed to that word''.'

Don adds, 'You can well imagine what that did for me! Immediately I was one hundred per cent free. And I trust I shall never be caught off guard again. Hallelujah.'

A third experience of deliverance took place at Torbay a couple of years after the second, Lady Faith Lees being the anointed vessel whom God used on this occasion. The meetings went on until two and three o'clock in the morning as the Holy Spirit, through the gifts of the Spirit, revealed needs.

Don still had times when he suffered depression, as old fears occasionally assailed him. Don says, 'It was more a case of "being afraid of being afraid".' The ministry of prayer and laying on of hands that he received at this time brought to a climax the work of deliverance that had been progressing since his conversion.

Don seldom has fears now. 'If I do, they are only transitory ones. Nothing that with God I am unable to handle,' he asserts.

A good illustration of the reality of this deliverance concerns his visit to Nairobi in 1975. Due to board the plane for home, the passengers were informed that the engine was leaking. There would be a delay.

Don settled down for a long wait. Five minutes later the call came to board. The trouble had been fixed!

Don confesses that he had a few queries in his mind as to the efficiency of that five-minute job, and African technology, but even so, he experienced no fear. He committed himself into the hands of the Lord, and settled down to enjoy the trip. Needless to say, Don and his companions are still around to tell the tale.

15

'Thy Loving Kindness'

Miracles of provision are part and parcel of a life of faith lived in the centre of the will of God. But every now and then something happens which seems to reveal the Father-heart of God in an extra special way.

Early in 1966, Don and Heather had begun to feel they really needed a car for their own use, instead of always being dependent on the team van. So together with Heather's mother they made it a matter of prayer and began to praise the Lord for the answer.

Putting faith into action, Don went down to the nearest garage and asked to look over the new cars. An eager salesman showed him around, and Don, feeling like a business man with a fat cheque-book in his pocket, grandly condescended to go home and 'think it over'.

Whitsun came around and with it the Whit. Convention. During one of the morning meetings a special love-offering was taken up for Don, but this one contained something more than money. Mixed up in the conglomeration of bank notes and loose change which amounted to about £30 they found a little piece of paper torn from the top of a sweet-bag. Scribbled across it was the brief message, 'A new car. Praise the Lord.'

'Well, praise the Lord,' Don responded when he saw it, and he spent the rest of the day waiting for something to happen. At long last, in the break between the afternoon and evening services, a gentleman walked up to

Don with a big smile on his face.

'Mr Double,' he greeted him, 'about your new car. What would you like? You can have any car on the market!'

Dumbfounded, Don gazed at the newcomer for a long moment. 'W-well,' he stumbled out at last, 'I'd like the one the Lord wants me to have.'

'But I don't know which one the Lord wants you to have,' returned the gentleman. 'All I know is He's told me to give you a new car.'

Visions of Rolls Royces and Bentleys flashed across the screen of Don's mind. Then more realistically, 'Well, to be honest, I was trusting the Lord for a Cortina Shooting Break,' Don replied.

'A Cortina Shooting Break?' exploded the other. 'You're an evangelist. You need something better than that!'

'Wow!' thought Don. 'This man has had a revelation. At least there is one person in the world who doesn't expect us to be riding around on a donkey's back, or in a car tied together with bits of string!'

Then aloud, 'Well, I've told you what I believe. It's over to you now.'

And that is how it came about that a few days later Don drove out of Park Lane in London with a Zephyr 6 Estate car, fully paid for, taxed and insured, and with a tankful of petrol. What did it matter that his coat pocket contained nothing but a few jingles of loose change? He felt like the son of a king—which of course he was.

Even the subsequent theft of the car could not eclipse the wonder of God's loving provision—though needless to say, its recovery was accompanied by much thanksgiving.

The following year, with the Good News Crusade now firmly based in St Austell, it did seem time that Don and his young wife should have a home of some description. They had in mind a small cottage down a back street, which in that area could still be rented for a couple of pounds a week. Unfortunately, a large waiting list disappointed their immediate hopes.

They begun to make their need a definite matter of prayer. Don particularly recalls the day when a friend, Pastor Sid Purse, knelt with them and prayed, 'Lord my brother Don needs a home. Please give him a house.' As in the case of the car, Don had not set his sights at any lofty level. He still had in mind the little cottage, and would have been content that God should somehow make one available. But the Lord had other plans.

Shortly after this, a man came up to Don and startled him with the announcement, 'The Lord has told me to give you a house.' 'Thank you very much,' Don replied gratefully, taking it for granted that the man owned property and would rent him a house.

'It's not built yet,' continued his new friend, 'and you can choose where you would like it.' Now Don was catching on. He was to be the owner of his own house! So they chose a site in St Austell and built a lovely three-bedroomed house looking out on thirty miles of Cornish coastline, with rolling hills behind and the township down in the valley. 'How gracious the Lord is,' Don thought as he saw the place taking shape.

'But then,' he calls, 'I received a visit from the devil. 'You're going to look a fool, aren't you?' the evil one began to insinuate. 'You've got a nice house. But you don't have any furniture to put in it. And no money to buy any either. Phew! What a dill!'

'Come to think of it, that's right,' Don found himself agreeing, picturing himself sitting in the middle of his new living room—on an orange box.

That little conversation, and momentary concession to the devil, predictably brought on an attack of unbelief. For four days Don lived in an agony of mind, wondering just what kind of a mess he had got himself into this time.

'Finally,' Don says, 'the Lord got through to me.' I was driving through St Austell, just near the Speedway Stadium, when the Holy Spirit said clearly, 'Don, if I could give you a house, don't you think that I could furnish it as well?' Well, that made sense. There and then, Don repented of his unbelief.

Within hours, a man came to Don and said, 'The Lord has told me to give you an automatic washing machine.' 'Hallelujah—clean clothes!' Don cheered. 'Lord, I'm going to trust you to furnish this house from top to bottom. No hire purchase. Everything paid for by the day it is dedicated.'

As money began to come in for furniture, Don and Heather started to look around for a refrigerator. In several places friends in the trade offered generous discounts of up to 16%, but each time Don felt the check of the Holy Spirit in his heart and did not commit himself.

One day, Don, Heather and Rhoda Martin went into Plymouth for shopping and decided to look over the refrigerators in a large store. While enquiring in the electrical department, they saw the very thing they were looking for being offered as a Star Bargain the following day with 33⅓% off. This was more than a bargain! It was practically a gift! At least, it would be for the customer fortunate enough to receive it, namely the first person there next day to claim it.

When Heather and her mother arrived sharp the following morning people were already standing at each door. Heather expectantly joined one of the queues. What if those six or so people in front of her, not to mention those waiting at all the other entrances, each wanted the same thing?

The doors finally opened and there was a mad rush into the store in all directions. Heather made speedily for the electrical department, and as the first customers burst in, the salesman looked up with a smile, pointed his finger at Heather and announced 'Your refrigerator, madam.' So Heather joyfully claimed her Star Bargain, paid her money, and went home to await delivery.

And so it went on. One thing after another was graciously provided. True, they waited a whole year for easy chairs, but all the basics were in place by the day of dedication. Only one bill was still outstanding as that day dawned—an item costing five pounds.

That morning they looked eagerly at the first post. Nothing. Then in the second delivery came a small parcel from Sheffield. Inside they found a picture text, 'The Lord will Provide,' and wrapped around it—a five pound note!

While the house was still being built, Don suddenly remembered another expense he would have to face. Rates! Shortly afterwards, while sitting in a conference meeting, next to Edgar Trout, during the last moments of the very last meeting, an elderly gentleman rose to his feet.

'The Lord keeps giving me a scripture,' he told them hesitantly, 'and I feel I should read it out.' Then he read from Matthew 17:27—'. . . Take the coin, and go and pay the rates and the taxes.' He sat down.

Edgar Trout, knowing nothing of Don's inner thoughts, dug his elbow into him.

'Brother Don. That's for you.'

'I know it is.'

'Stand up then, and testify.'

Don stood to his feet. 'Friends,' he said, 'I have just received my rates for my new house.'

Next morning, a man approached Don. 'Brother Don, the Lord has told me that when your rate bill comes in, you are to send it on to me.'

'Praise the Lord,' Don murmured.

'Not only that one, but all that follow,' the friend added.

'Bless you,' responded Don, 'and thank you, Lord.'

At that dedication of the house in March 1968 Edgar Trout looked out of the window at the beauty of the Cornish coast and raised his arms to God in praise—a gesture which found a response in the hearts of everyone present, as they reviewed the loving kindness of the Lord. 'And that was the last time I saw Edgar alive,' Don muses, for the Lord called their friend home shortly afterwards.

But some of the sweetest stories of God's tender care have nothing to do with cars or houses, but concern much smaller matters, for God even caters for his servants' innocent desires and preferences.

Don loves strawberries, and as his birthday falls in June, it has always been the custom in his home to enjoy strawberries on his birthday. In fact he has had them for his birthday every year that he can ever remember.

One year, being a wet summer, there didn't seem to be many strawberries on sale, and the few available were even more expensive than usual.

When Don's birthday came around the Rev. Oral Roberts happened to be holding his great Newport (Monmouthshire) Crusade, and Don attended, just one in a crowd of about seventeen thousand. During the day the thought crossed Don's mind a trifle wistfully, 'What a pity. This will be the first year of my life that I've not been able to have strawberries on my birthday.'

Between meetings in that vast stadium, Don unexpectedly came face to face with an acquaintance, a man whom he had met only about twice before, and one who knew nothing about Don personally.

'Hello,' the brother greeted Don pleasantly. 'Nice to see you. How are your crusades going?'

They chatted amiably for a few minutes about the Lord's work. Then suddenly the man put his hand into the bag he was carrying and produced a basket of strawberries. 'Here,' he urged, holding them out to Don, 'the Lord has just told me to give you these.'

Don's eyes widened in wonder. A birthday present from the Lord! He accepted the gift gratefully with something like awe. 'I wept,' he admits. 'How kind is the God we serve.'

Another similar incident took place more recently, but again reveals the Father-heart of God, who delights to give good things to his children.

Don is very fond of corn on the cob, which in England is quite expensive. One year Heather was able to buy some cheaply straight off a farm, and put it in the deep freeze to enjoy during the winter months.

The following year, due to a bad summer, there didn't appear to be any available, except at the freezer centres, and to buy it there would have been 'very expensive'.

'Well, I believe in prosperity, but not in extravagance,' Don comments.

One day that summer, while on the way to Cleveland for ministry, Don spotted a farm advertising corn on the cob at less than half the city price, provided you picked your own. 'Right, I'll go there in the morning and get some before going on to Fleet,' Don decided.

After arriving at the meeting place that evening, a lady mentioned to Don that there would be a women's meeting the following morning and they would very much like him to address it. Would he be willing?

'There goes my corn on the cob,' thought Don, but knowing he must 'seek first the kingdom of God,' he said he would be glad to speak.

Somewhere in the course of conversation that evening Don mentioned to his host how surprising it was to see corn on the cob advertised, in view of the unsuitable weather they had been having.

Next morning, unknown to Don, members of the family with whom he was staying went down to the farm and picked a hundred heads, and gave them to him as a gift before he left.

'Proof again,' he says, 'that if we put God first, then all these things will be added to us—including corn on the cob.'

16

Where the Action Is

As early as 1963 Don felt strongly that he needed a tent for his summer evangelistic work. He began to pray to that end, and in 1965 purchased his first two-hundred seater. Now they needed chairs and other equipment, not to mention a large van to carry it all.

Don challenged his supporters through *Ripened Grain* to each purchase one chair and take up the responsibility of praying for those who would sit on their chair during the crusades. He also had a conviction that he should buy good chairs, so that people could relax and not have to balance uncomfortably while listening to the gospel message.

Don put in his order for one hundred chairs, committing himself for £320 long before the money came in. After he had signed the contract he suffered a few days of doubt, wondering if he had been presumptuous, but he came through to faith, and took delivery in May. In due course all was amply provided, and Don held his first tent crusade in Huntingdon in August and September of the same year.

The Huntingdon Crusade, besides being the first to be conducted in a tent, was significant in other ways. At this time a young ex-sailor, David Adamson, together with Jette his Danish wife, joined Don's team, taking over from Brian Eastwell as crusade manager and youth director.

Don had met David in Cornwall a couple of years earlier while David was still in the navy, and apparently sensing the young man's potential, had invited him to attend the next Easter Convention at Ipswich.

Around Easter, David's ship came into Weymouth, but since it was under orders to be operational, no one was allowed ashore. Nothing daunted, Don wrote to the captain, expressing his conviction that God wanted David Adamson at Ipswich that Easter, and secured the needed permission.

At the convention, Don made David the songleader. It was there also that David met his future wife, a young nurse who together with another Danish friend frequently sang at Don's meetings.

In 1965 with the call of God upon his life, David obtained his discharge from the navy, married Jette, and several months later joined Don.

Although the couple remained on the team for only a year, afterwards serving as missionaries in Tanzania, this friendship became the link which subsequently took Don on many of his overseas evangelistic trips.

The Huntingdon Crusade also made history for Don, in that a young Anglican layman David Laycock received the baptism in the Holy Spirit. This young man went back to his home at Hemingford Grey and began to win people to the Lord. Among these were Mike Darwood, an agriculturalist, and his wife Muriel. When Don later came to a nearby Baptist Church for follow-up meetings, David Laycock attended together with several new converts, including the Darwoods.

The first night Mike Darwood didn't like the meeting at all. After the Anglican service to which he was accustomed, he found the freedom of worship somewhat disconcerting. Next evening he planned to stay away, the local prayer meeting furnishing him with a worthy excuse. Nevertheless something seemed to draw him, and as soon as the prayer meeting ended, he and his wife made their way to the Baptist Church, where Don's meeting had already begun.

The church was quite full, and they had to sit separately. But at the end of the meeting, when Don called for those desiring prayer to come forward, Mike went to the front, and to his surprise found himself kneeling beside Muriel.

Don addressed the seekers: 'Now, I'll tell you why you've come forward for prayer.'

'That's helpful,' Mike commented to himself, 'because I'm sure I don't know why I came out.'

'You've come to receive the baptism in the Holy Spirit,' Don continued. 'In a few moments I shall come and pray with you. And when I lay my hands on your head, you will speak with a new tongue.'

Mike had no idea what it was all about. Even so, the power and presence of the Lord was so real in the meeting, that before Don came to them, both he and Muriel had started to speak in other tongues. As Don came by he observed, 'No need to pray with you. You've got it.' Mike and his wife went home wondering just what they had got!

But that was only the beginning of many wonderful happenings in their lives, as other gifts of the Holy Spirit began to be manifest in their midst.

Over the next few years the Darwoods kept contact with Don, providing hospitality when he was in the district, and gradually becoming more actively involved in the crusades. In 1970 they moved to Cornwall as part of Don's permanent team. Mike not only became virtually Don's right hand man, but both he and Muriel now have a very fine ministry in their own right, and often accompany Don on his overseas crusades.

From the beginning of the tent ministry, Don prayed that his tent would be 'a spiritual maternity ward'. And so it has been through many years of crusading. Don says, 'We could count on one hand the night people have not been saved.'

Although not a few ministers of the gospel take the view that tent meetings belong to a past era, and that 'you just can't get people in these days', Don's experience has been quite the reverse.

The time arrived when the two-hundred-seater became inadequate and Don began to talk to the Lord about it. Before long one of his supporters felt the Lord wanted him to buy a new section for the tent and told Don so. The tent now grew to three-hundred-and-fifty capacity.

In course of time the need arose for a five-hundred capacity tent. They added another section. But it was still inadequate. By 1976 a new one-thousand-seater tent had been prayed into reality, and has since been increased to one-thousand-four-hundred seating capacity.

Around 1968 Don had occasion to call in at Post Green, the estate of Sir Thomas and Lady Lees, whom he had met earlier at Torbay Court.

Don's visit coincided with a conference day at their home, when the well-known American lady evangelist Jean Darnall was the speaker. During the meeting Jean Darnall announced a youth camp to be held at Post Green and mentioned the need of a tent.

The drawing room was packed to capacity when Don arrived, so he sat outside in the hall and did not hear the announcement. Later, Sir Thomas introduced Don to the preacher. Jean looked up with interest when she heard Don's name. 'Yes, I've heard about you,' she commented brightly. 'Sir Thomas tells me you have a tent that seats two hundred persons. That's just what I've been praying for. I believe you have to come to our youth camp.'

'Whoa—hold it,' Don thought, as he mentally put on the brakes. He didn't want to be rushed into anything precipitately on someone else's guidance.

'Oh er, well, sister, I'll have to pray about it,' he demurred. Jean proceeded expectantly to inform Don of the proposed youth camp dates. And would you believe it? They were the only dates in the whole year that Don had free.

Confirmation? 'Not necessarily,' thought Don. That was time set aside to spend with the family, of whom he reminded himself, 'I see far too little as it is.' No. Post Green would have to find another tent and another evangelist. But when Don began to pray about it with an open heart, the Lord said, 'Go.'

Faith and Tom Lees, appreciating the family situation, kindly encouraged Don to bring them along too. So in the end they all went—Heather, Nigel, Julia and baby Stephen.

In answer to prayer the Lord also sent in extra personnel to make up a full team for the camp. One of these, a minister on his way to Spain for a holiday, complete with a caravan, had a breakdown right near Post Green and couldn't go on. He became part of the ministry that year.

The camps continued annually with tremendous blessing, and although in due course Post Green acquired their own tent, Don's ministry continued to be a regular feature for several years.

17

Venturing Abroad

In 1964 Don received an invitation from Jette's church 'Ebenezer' in Copenhagen, to spend some time ministering in Denmark.

An itinerary was soon arranged and in October of the same year, with Heather, Rhoda Martin, Susan Love and Jette, Don made his debut in Copenhagen.

The first Sunday night in a Full Gospel Church in the suburb of Vanlose, facing a packed congregation, Don had his first experience of speaking through an interpreter. The Holy Spirit moved as in England, and in addition to several conversions, some were filled with the Holy Spirit. Others were healed of various infirmities, including the pastor's wife who found deliverance from insomnia and an over-tired heart. News of the miracle spread quickly, producing a spirit of expectancy wherever Don ministered.

Don had thoughts of returning to Denmark the following year, but the way did not open again until 1968, the occasion being the Adamsons' farewell prior to their departure for Tanzania.

As Don stood on the platform at Copenhagen Station, together with about a hundred Danish Christians waving goodbye to David and Jette, he felt a twinge of sadness that no church or organization in England had taken the Adamsons upon their heart to send them to the mission field.

At the same time the Holy Spirit spoke to Don and told him that he himself would go around the world and would preach the Gospel in many nations.

Don has been to Denmark again for ministry on several occasions since, also briefly taking in Holland, Sweden and Germany. On one of these visits Heather and he narrowly escaped serious injury in a car accident in Copenhagen. The driver, a young missionary on furlough, rushed the traffic lights while driving them to a meeting. The resulting collision threw Don about ten yards into the middle of the road. Dazedly picking himself up, Don caught a glimpse of pages of his loose-leaf Bible blowing down the street. 'You believe you're going to get the word of God spread around somehow don't you?' a friend joked later.

Don and his companions were taken to hospital where they were treated for bruises and mild shock. Shortly afterwards someone came to pick them up. 'How are you, brother Don?' the friend asked solicitously as he walked into the outpatient's department. 'Hallelujah, praise the Lord,' Don responded cheerfully. And in that spirit of victory the meetings went ahead as planned.

During Don's early visits to Denmark, he found most of the churches he attended to be quite bound by formalism. But by the time of his later visits an impressive change had developed. In permissive Denmark where pornography of every kind had been legalized the Spirit of God was raising up a standard against the evil.

Young people from the churches, forsaking their ritual and their formal choirs, were out on the streets witnessing for Jesus in the power of the Holy Spirit.

In some of the worst spots in the city hundreds of people would stand around listening to the Gospel message while drunks, and those addicted to all kinds of evil, would be kneeling on the pavement seeking the Lord.

As Don walked down one of these streets where every kind of filth and bestiality is offered to the public in 'live shows', he felt physically sick. Young participants, their faces distorted and mask-like, stood outside their places of employment seeking to lure in likely customers.

'Coming in?' one young zombi asked Don, in English.

'No thanks. I've got a live show of my own,' he retorted with distaste.

The young man's eyes fell on Don's 'Jesus' sticker.

'Oh, you're one of them,' he replied, turning away. He and his companions had good reason to know who 'they' were. Fifty or so young Christians would sometimes gather outside these places, praying and praising the Lord aloud. Then one would lift up a Bible in his right hand and pronounce the Lord's judgement against the evil practices going on inside. Something of the fear of God had already begun to fall on the neighbourhood, and some of the shows had actually closed down.

Don rejoiced to see the blessing and power that had come to so many of the churches as the renewal of the Holy Spirit had reached them. 'After all,' he emphazises, 'this is what the baptism in the Holy Spirit is all about.'

In 1968 the Holy Spirit impressed Don that He also had a ministry for him in the United States. Harry Greenwood arranged a meeting and in the autumn of that year, together with John MacLauchlan, Don made preparation to go.

Air tickets had already been purchased and everything seemed to be under control when suddenly a cable arrived from the USA cancelling the meeting. In spite of this setback, Don still felt strongly that they should proceed to America as planned. This leading was shortly confirmed both by a word from the Lord and also by the arrival of a gift in US dollars, the first Don had ever received in that currency.

On October 28th the two men flew to Chicago, arriving in the unfamiliar city without any plan of action and no contacts. What should they do now? They had nowhere to preach and only enough money for two nights in a hotel—and Don loathed hotels.

'Lord,' he prayed, 'you know how much I dislike hotels. Please get us into a Christian's home tonight.' (Don has since changed his views about hotels, but does love to stay in homes and have fellowship as he travels.)

Don had heard of Faith Tabernacle, Chicago. Now he felt impressed to look in the telephone book for that number. He phoned and explained who he was.

'Stay right there. We'll call you back,' a lady answered pleasantly. Don gave her the number of the public phone booth and about twenty minutes later the message came through, 'Someone will pick you up.' In a short while a car drew up outside the airport building and a lady leaned out and signalled to the two evangelists.

'Put your bags in the trunk,' she instructed in a slightly Norwegian accent, without checking as to whether they were the right men or not. Two Englishmen on their first visit to America were no doubt more conspicuous than they realized.

Somewhat awed by the strange circumstances in which they found themselves, and exceedingly weary after the flight and the time change, they climbed into the back of the car and said not a word. Their hostess, too, perhaps sensing their weariness, made no effort at conversation.

Arriving at her attractive American-Norwegian style house, she showed them their room, told them, 'You have a house meeting tonight,' and left them to rest.

Several hours later, refreshed and feeling more 'at home', they soon found that things began to thaw out. That evening as people began to arrive for the meeting, a large, overweight man breezed in, whom Don recognized immediately. He had seen him in a ministers' conference in Birmingham back in England—James Hosier, a man with a unique singing ministry.

Delighted to meet Don and his friend, James Hosier lost no time in setting up an itinerary for them which gave them thirty-nine meetings in the twenty-eight days available—days that were to be packed full of exciting happenings as they travelled from place to place in the flow of the Spirit's leading.

The following year, the way opened up again for Don to minister in the USA. This time John MacLauchlan was unable to accompany him, so Don approached Mike Darwood. Mike, who was still working as an agriculturalist, had become more involved in the work of GNC during the previous summer and had even begun to preach a little. Impressed with this ministry, Don saw in him a potential 'Timothy', and rang him one evening with his surprise proposal.

Overcoming his first negative reactions—his employers would never agree (in any case, what about his family, how could he leave them with no income for two months?)—Mike applied for unpaid leave. When he sought advice from his vicar on the wisdom of his decision, the Rev. D. E. Brown replied that in his opinion two months with Don would be better training than two years in a Bible College!

Consent soon came through from Mike's employers, and overcoming any final misgivings he set out on the great adventure which was to change the whole direction of his life.

'Don took me through a thorough apprenticeship, encouraging me step by step,' he recalls. Mike also discovered to his joy that when he preached, souls were saved. When he prayed for the sick, bodies were healed. He also discovered that God could meet his personal material needs and care for his family at home at the same time.

Don's third visit to America in 1972 took him together with Mike to Salem Gospel Tabernacle, Brooklyn, New York, a church with which they now have a very close relationship. This church is one of a group of churches within a fifty-mile radius, including Long Island, Staten Island, and parts of New Jersey, whose ministers meet together regularly for prayer and fellowship. These have given special recognition to Don's and Mike's ministries, and Don invariably visits 'Salem' first whenever he goes to the USA moving out from that fellowship for other ministry.

The thrilling stories of individuals who have been blessed through the USA visits are too numerous to enumerate, but one outstanding feature in America, as in other countries, always seems to be the number of 'chronic seekers' for the baptism in the Holy Spirit, who come into blessing without much effort under the anointed preaching and prayer ministry of Don and Mike.

Another interesting aspect of one of Don's visits to Salem Tabernacle was the time he prayed for every individual member of each family present. For many of the young people he prayed specifically for God's leading for their right partner in life.

In the summer of 1976 a young couple from the tabernacle turned up on Don's doorstep in St Austell and stayed with Heather and himself for several days. They were on their honeymoon, and declared they were one of the answers to his prayer. They added that Pastor Floyd Nicholson couldn't get away on holiday that year because he had so many weddings to take for the young people in his church!

In 1975 and 1976 Don and a full team visited Canada, their initial itinerary and contacts having been set up by their good friend the Rev. John Hutchinson. One of the outstanding memories of these visits was a crusade conducted at a little town called Marmora. Out of a population of under one thousand, four hundred attended nightly and many were saved, baptized in the Spirit or healed.

On the last night, when preaching, Don said in the spirit of prophecy, 'There are no grades of sin. Even if you have committed murder, God can forgive you, because there is no difference between murder and a white lie, in God's sight. The man who has murdered and the man who has told a white lie are both equally guilty. But both can receive forgiveness through Christ.'

Unknown to the team there was a man sitting in the congregation who had shot his wife. Awaiting trial but out on bail, he had told the prison chaplain, 'I am prepared to accept the state's judgement, but I cannot face the judgement of God.'

When Don gave the invitation that night, this man was the first down the aisle, and one of the team soon led him through to Christ.

Don sees his ministry in the USA and Canada as part of the fulfilment of God's message to him while in Denmark—that He would send him around the world with the Gospel.

Since 1968, every year's programme has included at least one overseas trip, and sometimes two or more, for Don and the team. In addition to the above mentioned countries, Don has already ministered in Tanzania, Kenya, Uganda, Greece, Japan and Chile, with invitations to New Zealand and other African nations awaiting God's timing.

18

To the Mission Fields

Don has always had a heart for overseas missions, but the time came when God challenged him to go in person for evangelistic and teaching ministry.

Invitations arrived from the Adamsons in Tanzania, and from the Rev. Godfrey Dawkins, a missionary in Kenya.

Don wrote in *Ripened Grain* in early 1970, 'No one really wants to leave his wife and family and be away for weeks, perhaps months on end. . . . But in the light of the cross . . . and realising the millions that are still in heathen darkness, there was only one answer I could possibly give—"Yes."'

When Don gave his answer, he still had a feeling he might be able to avoid going because of the expense involved. But before he had a chance to do anything about raising the money, God set His seal on the venture by sending in a substantial gift earmarked 'Tanzania'.

The remainder of the needed £1,000 came in steadily, and in October that year, together with George Telfer, a current member of his team, and Rhoda Martin, his mother-in-law, Don set out for East Africa.

As the great plane winged its way towards Nairobi, Don and his party had plenty of time to ponder the words of a prophecy given at a farewell rally prior to their departure: 'Watch for the rainbow.' What could it mean? Were they on the verge of some tremendous new blessing?

Don says, 'The Lord had quickened to me the scripture, 'I shall give thee the heathen for thine inheritance,' (Psalm 2:8) and I felt a great sense of mission.'

It was after 11 p.m. when the party arrived at Nairobi. As Don stepped off the plane and felt the warm air on his cheeks, and heard the buzz of unfamiliar voices around him, he felt almost as if he were treading on holy ground. He stood on the threshold of a new phase in his ministry, thrilled to be there in the centre of the will of God.

As they passed out of the customs shed, a mass of dark hands grabbed for their cases, as eager brown faces begged for the opportunity to carry them and earn a few coins.

Bewildered, Don and his companions glanced around them. With relief they caught sight of a familiar figure. 'So you've made it. This is Africa,' David Adamson greeted them warmly. He also introduced them to some other missionary friends, Ted and Esther Kent, and together they made their way to a guest house where they enjoyed a little fellowship together before settling down for the night.

A few hours later after a simple breakfast of tea, bread and butter and jam, the Good News Crusade trio piled into David's Land Rover and started for Itigi, David's mission station, seven hundred miles away. On the way out to Nairobi to meet the visitors, David, travelling alone, had suffered three punctures and also a leaking petrol tank. Now Don prayed there would be no further trouble with punctures on the return journey. In spite of the poor condition of the tyres, that prayer was answered.

But even so for Don and his companions from England, as yet uninitiated into things African, the journey through virgin bush country proved to be quite hair-raising.

The Land Rover pushed on for long hours through tropical bush, over 'roads that don't exist'. When they stopped now and then in some country town for petrol or refreshment, Don found himself looking around fearfully for a snake, and half expected a lion to suddenly come charging out of the bush.

Driving along, David relieved the tediousness by filling them in on local customs, and innocently regaled them with stories of tribes which still insist on the head of a man, or the tail of a lion, as a proof of manhood, before a youth can be married.

Later as they passed through mountainous areas, up steep inclines and down escarpments, David would nonchalantly pass comments such as, 'A bus went over there last week,' until Don seriously wondered if he would ever see his wife and family again.

Bright spots in the journey were stop-overs at two mission stations, with an opportunity to preach at a meeting in an African pastor's home. Then the nightmare journey began all over again.

On and on they travelled through the bush. Darkness had already fallen again but they pressed on through the night. Suddenly, while travelling on a precipitous mountain road, a rough jolt caused David to slam on his brakes. They had hit a wandering cow. It now lay across the narrow path, blocking their further progress.

This was Rhoda Martin's cue. Never at a loss, she alighted from the vehicle and laying her hands on the animal prayed expectantly. Within seconds, the cow staggered to its feet, briefly took its bearings, and trotted off into the night. With sighs of relief and much thanksgiving, the weary travellers continued on their way.

Next day, as they moved on through semi-desert

country towards the mission station where Jette and the native Christians eagerly awaited them, Don recalls feeling 'very depressed'. They seemed to be so far from civilization, and that same ghastly journey lay between them and everything he had ever held dear.

Their destination drew nearer. Now they began to smell rain, an unheard of thing at that time of the year. No rain was due for another two months at least. Yet in that arid country the scent was unmistakable. Sure enough, before long heavy drops began to spatter down so David had to put on his wind-screen wiper.

Meanwhile the locals waiting at the mission station were equally surprised and delighted at the sudden downpour. 'Oh, our guests are coming with blessings,' they shouted to each other joyfully.

After about thirty minutes the rain stopped as suddenly as it had started. Now, as David and his party turned left into the Itigi mission compound, a most beautiful rainbow met their gaze, circling the station, touching the ground from horizon to horizon. 'Wonderful! Just what God said through the prophecy,' murmured George, as they all gasped in admiration.

For Don, the rainbow held a special significance. It lifted the depression and restored his sense of joy and proportion. Through it he seemed to hear the voice of the Lord saying to him personally, 'I love you. I have sent you here. You are my child. My covenant promises are towards you. I will bless you.'

Word of the foreigners' arrival travelled quickly in the locality, and that night they held an unscheduled meeting when Don preached a simple message from Romans 1:16—the Gospel is the power of God unto salvation.

Later when Don invited the sick to come for prayer, two blind men moved forward. Conscious of the sea of expectant faces around him, Don couldn't help wishing that someone with some internal condition had been first. But as he looked to the Lord in humble dependence, his faith rose, and the two blind men were wonderfully restored. Several deaf also received their hearing that evening. Seeing the miracles, some Muslims who were in the congregation knelt on the dirt floor and, with tears dripping down their faces into the sand, received Jesus as their own Saviour. Thus began several weeks of outstanding fruitfulness as the Holy Spirit moved among them.

Meetings were held in primitive churches, in a jail, and out in the open among some who had never once before heard the Gospel preached.

At Dodoma they went into the market place and, setting up their loud speakers on the Land Rover, began to sing and testify and preach. Within minutes a great crowd had gathered, which quickly swelled to about a thousand people. Around two hundred prayed the sinner's prayer and scores were healed of all manner of infirmities.

Because of the excitability of the people and the danger of being mobbed, Don did not attempt to lay hands upon individuals. He asked those who believed that God would heal them to lay hands upon their own bodies in faith, while he prayed a mass prayer. After the prayer a queue of people streamed by, testifying one by one how the Lord had healed them.

One of the most outstanding testimonies concerned a woman who had come with a big open ulcer on her leg, which had been filled with sand and flies, in horrifying condition. During the prayer, the ulcer completely disappeared, leaving not so much as a scar.

One Sunday, Don and his party went with David to Wogo-go Plain. This was completely virgin territory, visited for the first time a few weeks earlier by native evangelists. To reach the area involved another arduous trip, travelling down steep escarpments and across river beds.

As the people listened to the story of Jesus out under a tree in one of the villages, many responded, and found life abundant. The team had also taken along a big bottle of sweets, and after the ministry was ended the children lined up to receive a share of the first western confectionery they had ever tasted.

At the Adamsons' mission station some days of special teaching for native evangelists were followed by 'Bible Week' when people came in from all points of the compass, some having travelled up to one hundred miles on foot with loads of food as well as children on their backs.

Spiritual blessings abounded and many were wonderfully healed. Don's hostess, Jette, also experienced a remarkable healing. While preparing for the evening meeting Don had received a word of knowledge that someone would be healed that night of a serious pain in the back. On the way to church he mentioned this to Jette.

'This will be the first time I've used the word of knowledge in Africa,' he pointed out. 'Will this translate into Swahili all right?'

Jette did not answer. Instead, she looked at Don wonderingly. 'Do you think it could be me?' she asked him. She related how she had injured her back when her son Mark was born. An arthritic condition had set in, which gave her constant pain. Although she had successfully hidden the trouble from her visitors, not wishing to make a fuss, it was in fact beginning to get well-nigh unbearable.

There and then they paused in their tracks while Don laid his hands on Jette's head and prayed for her. Healing was instant and complete.

All too soon the time came for the team to leave

Tanzania and proceed to Kenya. They travelled along the same route by which they had come, until they reached Moshi, one of the mission stations they had visited on the way out. Here they had the opportunity to record some programmes for Radio Tanzania, fulfilling a prophecy Don had received some time earlier that he would broadcast to a nation. Don and George both preached, and Jette and David sang.

Leaving Moshi, they took the road through the game park. Here Don and his party saw lions in their natural habitat for the first time.

Back in Nairobi again the Adamsons regretfully said farewell to the Good News Crusade team, handing them over into the good care of Godfrey Dawkins of the Trinity Fellowship, a Christian Youth Organization with ties with the Anglican Church.

In Kenya nineteen meetings were squeezed into eight days included youth rallies, church services, house meetings and Bible School classes. Mrs Martin with a special gift for personal work led two headmasters of schools to the Lord, as well as ministering to many others. George Telfer with his guitar was popular with the young folk.

The great climax came when twenty-three Anglican congregations gathered together for Sunday services. Most of the people arrived the night before and many slept out in the open under the stars.

The organizers had built a speakers' platform of bamboo with a canopy of shredded banana leaves. When the Good News Team arrived and Don stepped out of the car, they saw his height, and for several minutes consternation reigned! Then with great manoeuverings they adjusted the shade so that their honoured guest would not get a crick in his neck every time he stood to preach!

During the Kenya meetings, as in Tanzania, several

blind people received their sight, adding up to a total of seven. One of these, Gerson Nyangaga of Ramula Parish, Kenya, had been blind since 1966. Don met him again on a subsequent visit and found him still healed and giving glory to God.

Statistics do not tell the whole story, but this first of Don's East African crusades resulted in about six hundred professed conversions; three hundred testimonies of miraculous healing; and over one hundred who received the baptism of the Holy Spirit.

Don has a real sense of call to East Africa, and he or a member of his team has been back for ministry every year since, to one or the other of the two countries, and has also ministered in Uganda. On several occasions members of Don's visiting team have stayed on after Don returned, for several months of prolonged service.

Highlights of subsequent visits to Kenya have been the Diocesan Retreat in 1971, presided over by the Right Rev. James Mundia, Bishop of Maseno North, when clergy from four hundred congregations were present; also conventions in Kikuyu and Mombasa in 1972 together with his then seventeen-year-old son Nigel, and Jean Darnall. On this occasion there were also appearances on Voice of Kenya television and radio, and finally a united Catholic and Protestant charismatic service at Kenyatta College, University of Nairobi.

Concerning this final service, Don wrote, 'If you had told me that my third visit to Africa would have ended up with me holding hands with a priest on one side and a mother superior on the other, I would never have believed you.'

In 1974 Don made a return visit to Tanzania. David Adamson and his wife, at this time working in the capital city of Dar-es-Salaam, invited Don for a city-wide crusade. David had written earlier, 'Every door is wide open, and we are reaping what others have sown. It is harvest time . . . we have already reached thousands of souls. Whether it has been in the open air or in the secondary schools, God has blessed, and I believe we are on the verge of a great breakthrough.'

Into this ripened field came Don and his team. The dates of the Dar-es-Salaam crusade coincided with the Muslim feast of breaking the fast (Ramadan), so was a public holiday. The crusade site was also a piece of public ground where the Muslims were celebrating, complete with a great fun-fair.

As a result, a large percentage of the Muslims living in Dar-es-Salaam, as well as thousands of other non-Muslims, either came to the meeting or heard the preaching over the public address system.

Although Muslims are notoriously opposed to Christianity, David Adamson reports that there is not the opposition of the past, and that the young people especially are very open.

During the four-day crusade an estimated fifty thousand people heard the gospel, as many as fifteen thousand in one service alone. Several thousand decisions were recorded and tremendous miracles of healing took place, including twenty-five deaf people whose hearing was restored. Many of those receiving healing had made no commitment to Christ at this point, yet God in his compassion and mercy demonstrated His love and power.

Mike Darwood who shared in the ministry with Don reported in *Ripened Grain:* 'Hundreds were freed from demon powers. . . . One young boy, ten years old, called on the name of the Lord, who straightened, lengthened, and strengthened his withered arm so that he was able to use it for the first time. A man paralysed from the waist down . . . was able to walk after prayer in the name of Jesus. Many were released from curses put on

116

them by witch-doctors, and greatest miracle of all, thousands were released from the worship of false gods. . . .'

One afternoon while Don was on the platform and Mike down among the crowd, an Asian gentleman approached Mike enquiring, 'Are you a colleague of Don Double's?' He then told an amazing story.

Four years previously when Don on his first missionary trip to Tanzania had stopped at the town of Dodoma and preached in the market place, this man had stood with his ten-year old daughter in the crowd. Blind from birth, she had never been able to attend school. As prayer was offered the child laid her hands upon her own eyes and was instantly healed. Since then her father had sent her to school in India, where she had made up in four years all the schooling she had formerly missed. 'I just wanted you to know,' the father told Mike gratefully.

By way of follow-up after the Dar-es-Salaam crusade, they showed a film called *The Messiah* made at Post Green and brought out to Tanzania by Don at David's request.

The church used for the film show soon filled up to capacity with crowds outside craning their necks through the windows to get a glimpse of the picture.

Emotional and uninhibited, the African audience wept and wailed aloud at the crucifixion of Jesus. When He arose from the grave they clapped and cheered—a never-to-be-forgotten scene for the visitors from England.

In 1976 Don visited Tanzania again for evangelistic crusades. Multitudes heard the Gospel and three thousand people publically confessed Christ as their Saviour, including several Muslims.

One Muslim, having heard the message and seen the miracles, went home, telling himself it was all a load of nonsense. He then became so convicted that he returned through the darkened streets at great personal risk. He called at the Swedish Free Mission Church, which together with David Adamson had sponsored the crusade, and gave his heart to Christ. The following Sunday morning he testified publicly to his salvation and even started preaching. Philemon, the pastor, finally had to pull at his shirt tails and tell him to stop when he had had twenty minutes!

Another mass crusade was held in the grounds of a school for the blind, at Tabora. One night five or six deaf people came forward for prayer.

Don lined them all up facing the platform. After he prayed for them he said, 'Now, I believe God has opened those deaf ears. I want you to turn round facing the congregation with your backs toward me so that you can't see my lips. I'm going to tell you what to do, and I want you to follow my instructions.'

Don then told them to stand on the right leg. Then on the left. 'Now raise your right arm,' he continued, 'now your left arm.' As the formerly deaf people obeyed him with ease, the crowd went crazy with delight.

Such scenes were repeated wherever they went. In a place called Mshamba, a village composed of poor huts and a few shops surrounded by banana trees, they set up their amplification system and preached from a wooden platform in the village square.

Some village lads who had gathered in an accustomed spot, on a wall on the edge of the square, responded to the intrusion into their territory by laughing and mocking—the first time Don had ever encountered open mockery of the Gospel in Africa.

Unknown to the team, down in the crowd a man supported by rough crutches stood listening to the message. A former polio victim, he was paralysed from the waist downwards. At the end of the message and the prayer for salvation, this man heard Don say that he would pray for whose who believed God would heal them.

'Put your hands on your own sick body while I pray,' Don instructed. 'Ask the Lord to heal you and then stop asking and begin thanking Him. After that, start doing whatever you were not able to do formerly.'

While Don was still speaking and before he even had a chance to pray, this man touched the Lord by faith and began to do what he hadn't been able to do—he put down his crutches and walked.

When testimonies were invited, he was the first to bound up on to the platform. Jumping up and down and waving his arms in great excitement in front of the microphone, he shouted that he had been healed.

The mockers on the wall stared in amazament, their jaws gaping. The last Don and his party saw of them, they were crowding around the former paralytic whom they all knew well, unable to deny the evidence of their own eyes.

Another highlight of this same trip was a visit to the Burundi Refugee Camp. There Don ministered at a communion service where, with a congregation of sixteen thousand, they used fifteen gallons of communion wine, and a whole sackful of bread.

Don also shares with the Adamsons in a burden for the island of Zanzibar, which is only twenty minutes' flying time from Dar-es-Salaam. David and Jette's original call had been to Zanzibar, but with a pro-Maoist-type government it had remained a closed door. Even the Bible Society had been unable to get in.

When Don went to Tanzania in 1974 he began to say to David, 'Come on, brother, we've got to do something about Zanzibar.' David says, 'As usual, Don began to pump faith into me.'

In a couple of places where they had special meetings for evangelists, Don made the announcement, 'If there is anyone here who feels a call of God for Zanzibar, please let Brother Adamson know.'

Sure enough, shortly after Don had returned to England, David received a letter from a young evangelist by the name of Yohanna. David subsequently met him in Dar-es-Salaam and, together with the pastor of the Swedish church, made plans to visit the forbidden island.

The three men obtained visitors' passes, flew to Zanzibar and booked into a hotel. There they sat down to discuss the next move. Believing that God's time had come, they decided at David's suggestion not to do anything underground, but to go straight to the authorities and request permission for their activities.

This they did, explaining, 'We are Christians from the mainland out looking for lost sheep. We have books and tracts we would like to distribute.'

'Why not?' came the mild official response. So they went through the whole area freely distributing literature, talking to people personally, and even doing a little open-air preaching.

Yohanna further extended his stay, and with a promise from Don in England that the Good News Crusade would raise his support for a year, he began to look for a place to settle.

There is now a small church in Zanzibar, and the first converts have been baptized.

In 1975 Don, together with Mike Darwood, visited a very different type of mission field—Japan. Two countries could scarcely present a greater contrast than Tanzania and Japan.

Sophisticated and materialistic, Japan has never experienced a major breakthrough spiritually. Statistics at meetings generally speaking have to be counted in fifties, tens, and even units, rather than in hundreds or thousands.

According to a 1976 Gallup poll, the Japanese are the most agnostic people in the non-communist world, with only 44% believing in a deity of any kind.

Yet paradoxically, idolatrous customs form the warp and woof of the whole social structure, making it difficult for individuals to take a stand for Christ without opposing and upsetting family members near and far.

Way back in the days when Don had worked with Vic Ramsey and his team, God had spoken to him about going to Japan some day. A number of years later an Australian missionary, Lionel H. Thomson, working at that time in the north of Japan, received a copy of *Ripened Grain* sent by a friend in England. Lionel liked what he read, wrote to Don, and a friendship developed.

In 1972 the Good News Crusade raised several hundred pounds to purchase a tent for Lionel's evangelism in Japan. And in May 1973 Don and Mike arrived in Tokyo aboard an Egypt Air flight, for a month's ministry in various parts of the country.

Don arrived with an upset stomach and did not feel really well for at least a week after his arrival, which perhaps partly accounts for the fact that he never did exactly fall in love with Japanese cuisine.

Following several small house meetings in Tokyo, Don and Mike together with Lionel Thomson, visited several cities in the south of Japan; Tenryuu, Nagoya, Kyoto and Kobe, ministering in a variety of churches and house meetings, before flying north to the island of Hokkaido.

In the city of Hakodate, a very live Four Square Church welcomed the visitors. It was pastored at the time by David Masui. Several outstanding miracles of healing took place during their short stay there. A young man who had been deaf in one ear since childhood, due to the removal of an ear-drum at the age of six years, had his hearing perfectly restored. A middle-aged lady who had been in hospital for several months with generalized arthritis also received a mighty touch from the Lord. She literally ran around the church with joy as she demonstrated her deliverance.

These miracles, together with various other healings, brought in six new enquirers to the church the following Sunday morning—a fairly rare occurrence in Japan.

From Hakodate the men travelled further north to the cities of Sapporo and Iwamizawa, where other meetings had been arranged. Attendances were not large in spite of wide door-to-door visitation, but the Christians in each place were encouraged and some experienced the Lord's touch of power upon their bodies as well as upon their spirits.

Wherever Don went in Japan, his size together with his name always seemed to raise a laugh. The Japanese are familiar with the British word 'double' having incorporated it into the Japanese language. They know about double beds, double ramen (a double-sized package of instant noodles) and double-punch. Consequently, whenever Don was introduced, side by side with his diminutive interpreter, as 'Mr Double', someone usually managed to quip that he was well named.

The real highlight of the Good News Crusade team's visit to Japan proved to be the three-day seminar for missionaries, pastors and other believers, held at the Christian Centre in Sapporo City, the capital of Hokkaido.

Studies from 1 Corinthians, chapters 12 and 14, on the nine supernatural gifts of the Holy Spirit, not only opened the eyes of many to a new breadth and depth of ministry, but also became the text of Don's first teaching booklet *Life in a New Dimension*. This book, prepared from transcripts of the taped messages, has subsequently sold thousands of copies in England and around the world, blessing multitudes with its practical down-to-earth teaching.

Don and Mike returned from Japan glad to have had a small part in reaching the Japanese for Christ, and acknowledging that probably their greatest contribution was to encourage the missionaries and Christian workers to reach out themselves for the manifestation of the gifts of the Holy Spirit.

Mike returned to Japan for three weeks in company with a young evangelist Simon Matthews, in February 1977, and the team continues to carry a concern and burden for that needy land.

19

Expansion

During the early years of the Good News Crusade, Don's team remained fairly fluid, with young men and women joining him for a year or two before moving on to other avenues of service. But from 1970 onwards a more permanent team began to emerge, and the whole pattern of the GNC's ministry has developed round the varied gifts these fellow workers contribute.

In the summer of 1970 sixteen-year-old David Abbott, a lad who had been saved as a child at Don's first tent Crusade in 1965, now joined the team. Only intending to stay about a year, this young man originally came in with a ministry of 'helps' doing many of the jobs which had formerly been performed by Pop Booth; and also assisting Heather with children's meetings.

But David stayed on, became equipment manager, took charge of the film unit, and in addition matured into a talented children's evangelist.

Besides regularly heading up the children's work at tent crusades, camps, and conventions in England, David has also spent two prolonged periods in Kenya, working with the Trinity Fellowship, and ministering in schools and colleges there; and he has also ministered in the USA.

Under his gifted leadership the children's department of the Good News Crusade has become an important facet of the whole work. David believes not only in bringing children through to salvation, but in leading them on into the power of the Holy Spirit. Many of these younger members of the body of Christ who have passed through his hands have been baptized in water, baptized in the Spirit, taken part in their own communion services and have ministered the gifts of the Spirit to one another.

If this somewhat unusual development raises questions in the minds of adults, the answer seems to lie in the word 'reality'. The Good News Crusade believes that provided the child has a genuine encounter with Jesus Christ there is nothing to fear.

In 1973 Miss Ann Timms joined David in the children's work, until part-time team member David Laycock claimed her as his bride. Even after that Ann continued part time whenever opportunity allowed. The Laycocks still have close contact with the Good News Crusade, and although no longer actual team members, they do have a supporting ministry.

Julia, Don's daughter, also began to take an increasingly active part in the children's ministry as she entered her teenage years.

In addition to David Abbott, the year 1970 saw two other permanent additions to the team, with the move of Mike Darwood and his wife Muriel to St Austell.

Mike's preaching soon developed along the line of a Bible-teaching faith-building ministry. Originally designated 'Crusade Manager' he is now known as 'Director of Counselling'. In addition to training the counsellors for crusades, he deals with an expanding counselling postal ministry. Scores of people have been saved, restored and healed through this pastoral caring by post.

Since 1971 Mike has been the editor of *Ripened Grain* (now assisted by Heather Double and Robert Parkinson as co-editors) and has also produced several popular

Bible-study books, *Receiving Power* (translated into Japanese, Spanish, and at least one Chinese dialect); *Christ's Healing Ministry Today: What Doth Hinder Thee?* (dealing with problems of unreality and defeat in the Christian life); and *Discipleship: The Daily Walk*.

Muriel, too, soon fitted in at St Austell as prayer secretary and librarian. She is responsible for sending out the monthly confidential prayer letter to hundreds of partners belonging to the Prayer Fellowship, keeping the lists up to date, compiling prayer requests, and a host of other duties.

Muriel is also active in the crusades, sometimes involved in counselling, sometimes at the bookstall. She also addresses ladies' meetings from time to time and has accompanied the team to both Canada and East Africa.

The next person to join the team was Daphne Allen in 1971 as Don's personal secretary, fulfilling a call to full-time service received seventeen years earlier, and filling the gap left by Don's former secretary Sue Love after she became Mrs Mike Heathcote.

During 1973 and 1974 three more secretarial ladies were added to the work; teenager Barbara Woodhouse, who in 1976 became Mrs David Abbott; also Rosemary Ellison and Pat Smallridge (now married to Mike Darwood's brother).

Barbara began by managing the bookshop at St Austell in place of Janet Robinson (who had taken over for a few months after Sheila Balmforth left) but now travels with the team in a secretarial capacity. Pat also worked in the bookshop, and was mainly responsible for the mail-order department, while Rosemary became Conference Secretary.

Each of these ladies takes her turn in travelling to crusades, and has a part in counselling and a variety of other ministries.

Easter 1973 saw another addition to the team in the person of eighteen-year-old Simon Matthews. Saved under Don's ministry in Cornwall several years earlier, Simon had joined the Par Gospel Church and with Don's encouragement had been having good experience in witnessing and preaching for over two years.

Now, from having been in charge of the youth outreach at the church, he became instead Youth Director on the Good News Crusade team. During the several years that have passed since then, Simon has developed a vital ministry, particularly (though not exclusively) to the under-thirty age group. Simon also speaks at senior schools, universities and colleges all over England and has ministered in Denmark, Africa, the USA, Canada and Japan. In March 1977 he became Don and Heather's son-in-law when he married their daughter Julia.

In 1972 Don met Tony Mettrick, a young and talented organist, and invited him to join the team. For several years Tony served in a temporary capacity continuing his regular employment as a professional musician, in between camps and crusades. Then, to everyone's delight, in 1976 Tony came in full time. He has since added another member to the team by marrying; his wife's name is Carol.

The gradually enlarging team and the proliferation of ministries meant that the GNC was outgrowing its premises on the second floor over the tailor in Fore Street. Happily, at just the right time, they were able to obtain the lease on the third floor, and have subsequently obtained part of the first floor as well.

In 1975 Don and the team began to pray about opening a second bookshop. The Lord had just the right contracts ready and they were able to lease a small shop in Hereford, near the Welsh border.

Known as the Book and Card Centre, the shop had formerly been owned by a Brethren gentleman. Now

127

due to retire, he had been praying for a Christian buyer. Barbara Woodhouse went down to get the shop going, and then the Lord called John and Joy Lydden of Bexhill, Sussex, to take over the work, as part of the Good News Crusade team.

Shortly after the opening of the Hereford store, Don and the others had a strong leading that there should be a third shop. Within a short time they had taken over a small store in Exmouth on the Devon coast. Started originally by a local Christian lady, the shop is situated not far from Haldon Court Hotel, where the Good News Crusade participate in renewal conferences every New Year and in the autumn.

When the GNC took over, the Lord called Miss Janet Robinson to manage the shop temporarily, and she continued until early in 1979. Harry Pridmore, a former computer operator, is now the manager at Exmouth, while Tony Mettrick supervises all three bookshops, in addition to his ministry in music. The Good News Crusade see their shops not as businesses, but as ministries, and the profits are used for the further spreading of the Gospel around the world.

In addition to the main team and the bookshop staff, the GNC have members engaged in outreach of a different kind. Since 1968 David and Ann Scott of Hemingford Grey, near Cambridge, have made their home the centre of the tape ministry.

Heather originally pioneered this aspect of the work, carrying the tapes around in a small suitcase. But as the demand increased it became clear that the work required more concentrated attention. There are now three full-time workers in this department; Ann Scott, Pat Grantham and Pam Reid. These three ladies maintain a busy schedule as they seek to keep up with the demands of the Tape Library.

After a crusade or convention, forty or fifty tapes will

arrive at the Scotts' residence, all of which have to be duplicated, named, added to the library, and orders sent out.

Originally, most tapes were borrowed and only a few sold, but in recent years the trend has been reversed with most people buying their tapes and only a few borrowing.

Along with the expansion of the Good News Crusade team, Don's own family expanded too, which meant that Heather was less able to travel than in the earlier days. Joel Gideon arrived in March 1972, followed the next year by Faith Sharon in April, so with Stephen then already seven years old her hands were full. However, Heather continued as treasurer of the GNC and rejoiced to see the many ministries which once fell to her taken over by others as each department expanded.

Heather is still in demand as a ladies' meeting speaker whenever her schedule permits, and has more latterly begun again to accompany Don on some of his overseas trips.

The eldest son Nigel, who for several years had a ministry with the team on a part-time basis, heard the call of God to missionary service while on a visit to Africa with his father. He is now in Tanzania with his wife Barbara and baby son Matthew, setting up a Christian Printing Press, and is deeply involved in the work of renewal in that land. Nigel and Barbara are regarded as full-time team members and part of the Good News Crusade overseas outreach.

The yearly schedule of the GNC is a well rounded one, which includes aggressive evangelism, the healing ministry, solid convention-type teaching, and missionary sorties abroad.

One outreach which has become a very popular part of the yearly programme is known as Teens' and Twenties' Weekends. Don had felt a burden to get closer to the young people and their needs and shared his thoughts with John Hutchinson of Torbay Court Conference Centre. Believing the Lord was in it they arranged the first Teens and Twenties' Weekend for January 19th-21st, 1973.

With a minimum of advertising the conference centre filled up to capacity, and Don describes that first youth weekend as 'an outstandingly wonderful success'. Now Teens and Twenties convene in several different areas each year.

According to Simon Matthews, who has the main responsibility, the weekends are usually heavily booked, often with waiting lists. They are run as cheaply as possible, and the guests are mainly single young people, the majority being already professing Christians.

The programme, which commences with the Friday evening meal followed by the first meeting, is fairly hectic, especially for the leaders who between meetings and often late into the night will be involved in counselling.

Many of the guests, although they may come from sound evangelical churches, are untaught in such practical matters as the dangers of the occult, the unequal yoke, and many other important issues. Much uncleanness and selfishness is dealt with, and many experience the baptism in the Holy Spirit during these vital weekends.

But probably the most popular of all the GNC outreaches in recent years has been the Family Camp held during August at Blaithwaite House, Wigton in Cumbria.

Owned by the Rev. Dennis Donald, Blaithwaite House is a large old fashioned country residence set in two-hundred-and-fifty acres of farm and woodland. Guests for the camp may enjoy the comfortable hotel-type facilities, or they may bring their own tents or caravans and camp in the grounds. The main meetings convene in the GNC tent.

The Blaithwaite camp began as Jean Darnall's project in 1970. In 1971 she invited Don to co-operate, bringing his tent along. The following year, Jean had other commitments, so Don took over and the week-long camp has become a yearly favourite.

Although 'Blaithwaite' is sponsored by the Good News Crusade, there is now also a big planning team made up of Christian leaders from all over the country. These, together with an army of camp counsellors and advisers, meet for a special weekend to plan and pray for the camp.

The several hundred campers divide up into units of about fifty to seventy people. Each unit has its own adviser together with his wife, plus about six counsellors. The counsellors are divided up among the various units for the sake of personal contact, but obviously the counselling ministry crosses unit boundaries.

The camp programme is full and varied—morning devotions under the trees (weather permitting); morning teaching sessions and seminars with various subjects from which to choose; youth meetings; evening rallies followed by 'unit devotions', when opportunity is afforded to testify and share more intimately than in the larger gatherings.

The children are catered for too with their own special meetings and a nursery for both the little ones and the babies. At night the children are put to bed by the 'baby patrol' while parents attend the evening service unhindered.

Afternoons include coach trips to Cumbria's beauty spots, sporting events, and unit presentations of drama and singing.

Blaithwaite Camp has several other popular events, one of these being the morning reserved for family ministry. Don himself always speaks at this meeting, and at the end prays for every person present.

First he calls out all the husbands. After he has prayed for them, he calls for the wives. Don prays for them, and then has the husbands pray for their own wives, and the wives for their husbands. Following this, other family members join their parents and minister to each other, in some cases seeking to put right attitudes which have long been wrong between them.

Finally Don prays for all the single people, for widows and for widowers. No one is left out. The week always ends with a great communion service on Friday night.

Not surprisingly most people find Blaithwaite Camp an exhilarating experience, with its heady blend of worship, teaching, fellowship, fun and relaxation.

By 1976 the attendance had climbed to 1,250 and in 1979 was fully booked five months before the event. No wonder that in 1977 a new family camp had to be added. On July 30th, six hundred people gathered at Chadacre Agricultural Institute in Bury St Edmunds, Suffolk, for a week of Blaithwaite-type ministry and blessing.

Life-changing experiences, to which nearly three hundred testified on the last night, included salvation, renewal, healing, deliverance and family reconciliations —all ample justification for the further addition to the Good News Crusade's still burgeoning programme.

20

Don the Evangelist

Since that distant evening when as an inexperienced and immature young man, Don held his first evangelistic meeting in a village hall in Suffolk, the angels have been kept busy recording and rejoicing over the thousands of changed lives that have passed under his ministry.

Don still cannot write well, nor spell properly, but with the help of the Holy Spirit he has learnt to read the Bible and virtually overcome the misfortunes of his early years.

Noting the rapt expressions on the faces of his student congregation as he preached one afternoon at a Christian Union meeting at Downing College, Cambridge University, Don chuckled inwardly, 'Lord, you certainly have a sense of humour. If they only knew!'

In the early days of his ministry, Don didn't have many sermons. Before his first full-time crusade in Jersey in 1961, he confided to a friend that he feared he might run out of material before the two weeks were over.

This same friend comments, 'I found his preaching quite plain. But he believed in using what he had, and in doing with all his heart whatever God told him to do.'

Not surprisingly, as Don's ministry developed and matured over the years, opinions concerning his preaching have changed.

One Anglican minister declares, 'Don has such an anointing upon him you can just go on listening and you don't notice the time. Even after a four-hour service I could go right back and take it all over again.'

The Rev. Elmer Darnall, husband of Jean Darnall and principal of the Christian Life Bible College, while advertising his school in a public meeting mentioned that one of the subject taught was homiletics, adding by way of illustration, 'If you want to hear a well-nigh perfect homiletic preacher, you should hear Don Double.' Whereupon Don, who was present in the meeting, turned to his wife and queried in a loud stage whisper, 'What's one of them?'

Having discovered homiletics as a by-product of his quest for sermons, Don has recently begun to teach the subject in some of his seminars on the Teens' and Twenties' weekends, and at camps and church meetings.

'Homiletics do not exclude the anointing and direction of the Holy Spirit,' he emphasizes; 'on the contrary, they make it easier for the Holy Spirit to work through us to our hearers.'

'From the beginning, Don was a worker rather than a mystic,' comments another friend. 'While many seemed to be waiting on the Lord ad infinitum, to receive a special anointing, here was someone who knew his call, relied on the promises in the Word, and got on with the job. Inevitably, any connection with Don meant you were put to work. To be honest he would sometimes be quite demanding.' This testimony is borne out by other friends and associates.

'I don't know another crusade team that works as hard as Don Double's team,' says Vic Ramsey. Don himself tells his new young workers, 'I promise you lots of work and no wages,' and by all accounts he keeps his promise.

A born leader, Don has also a gift for training others.

Many young workers have passed through his team on a temporary basis, going on to other fields of service, better equipped and more mature than when they joined him.

Don seems to have an ability to recognize a person's gift, and then exposes him to the opportunity to use it. Much of his training method consists of encouragement and example.

During David Adamson's first crusade with Don he was responsible for the 'Faith Class'. After three nights, David felt he had exhausted his fund of spiritual insights. 'Don, I can't preach any more', he gasped next day, 'I've told them all I know.' 'Well, from now on it's going to be the best,' Don responded confidently, and David gratefully recalls that from then on he really began to develop as a preacher.

Concerning this period with Don, David adds, 'I saw him as he prayed; I saw him as he ministered; I saw him on the mountain; I saw him as he cried; I saw him fasting; yes, I saw him practising exactly what he preached.'

Simon Matthews adds, 'Don has been more than a trainer. He has been like a father to me.' Even before Simon joined the team he recalls how Don encouraged him to run a crusade himself, with the help of some of the young people in the church at Par.

On the second evening of the youth crusade, Simon preached for the first time, while Don sat in the congregation listening. When Simon made the appeal and seven or eight youngsters came forward for salvation, Don jumped to his feet, praising the Lord and weeping for joy.

In matters of doctrine, Don seeks to remain true to the Word of God. He does not favour the kind of teaching and preaching that begins with an idea, which the preacher then proceeds to back up or defend with Scriptures taken out of context. Don believes in preaching what the Word says, not what we want it to say, and in an age in which new emphases, spiritual fads, and even heresies are legion, his desire is to keep a balance.

Don admits that in the early days of his ministry, he found himself somewhat susceptible to such influences, and became entangled on several occasions. Happily, he did not remain involved.

Don says, 'I regard extreme teachings as "cul-de-sacs" in the Christian's pathway. There is only one way to go on with God, and that is to come back out of the cul-de-sac the way you went in.' Extreme emphases, he believes, produce exclusivism, 'which,' he asserts flatly, 'is not of God.'

On one occasion when he found himself on the way down a cul-de-sac, Arthur Wallis, recognizing what was happening, invited Don to his home to pray and counsel with him.

Don says, 'God really got through to me. He spoke to me and said, "The only place of safety is to recognize the whole body of Christ—every single member." If you recognize every member of the body you can receive ministry from them and you won't ever cut yourself off from them, no matter who they are, or to what church they belong.'

At that time, the Lord also drew Don's attention to Romans 8:14—'For as many as are led by the Spirit of God, they are the sons of God.'

The Lord showed Don that since the Holy Spirit is a Spirit of unity, He will always lead people to the body of Christ. Never away from it. Don says, 'I received a tremendous deliverance through that word from God, and I've never been down a cul-de-sac since.'

When it comes to questions within the charismatic movement, as to the rights and wrongs of staying in the denominational churches or withdrawing to form house groups, Don will not take sides. He says, 'When people ask me, "Are you a come-outer, or a stay-inner?" I answer, "Neither! I'm a do-what-God-sayser!" There are times when it is right to come out, and there are situations where it is right to stay in. You can stay in and be wrong. And you can come out and be wrong. It's a case of "What is God saying to me in this circumstance?"'

Another principle Don seeks to follow in his ministry he learned through the teachings of the Rev. Oral Roberts—'Find out which way God is moving and move with Him.'

Don says, 'When I go into an area, I want to know what God is doing there. I don't take with me a new idea or a favourite hobby horse, or a preconceived notion that God must work the same way He did in the last place. I like to be sensitive and discover what God is doing locally, and move in that. Sometimes it may be with historic churches, sometimes with house fellowships, but these days it is usually with both together.'

Don learnt this lesson by bitter experience. In one of his finest crusades in Cornwall, God produced a thriving church of nearly a hundred people, out of a population of about two thousand. 'Then,' Don recounts, 'we tried to bring them into what God was doing in another place. It was like trying to get blood out of a stone. The work dwindled down to a handful. When the mistake was recognized, we put it right, and God graciously began to build it up again.'

In many of Don's meetings the gifts of the Spirit operate quite freely, especially the gift of the word of knowledge. A need or a sickness will be made known to the evangelist in the Spirit. Then the person concerned, after identifying himself as the one to whom it applies, will be prayed for, and frequently an instantaneous healing results.

But the Good News Crusade meetings are by no

means stereotyped. Seeking to be sensitive to the leading of the Holy Spirit, they seldom do the same thing two nights running.

Across the years, Don's whole method of conducting crusades has developed and matured as he has pursued excellence. Every year during the short English summer, Don holds three or four major tent crusades, usually lasting about seventeen days each. Most of the crusades now are by invitation, though in some cases Don will take the initiative in seeking an opening into some area where he feels the call.

All major crusades are planned as much as eighteen months ahead, with careful attention given to the building up of a local team of helpers, including even a catering unit.

Mike Darwood visits the inviting churches, showing slides of a previous crusade so that they can get a picture of what is involved. He goes again several more times in the ensuing months, to form the local working party. David Abbott and Simon Matthews also go and talk about the youth and children's work.

Regular prayer is encouraged and three pre-crusade rallies are planned when non-team speakers are invited, the aim being to contact Christians of various persuasions, with a view to unitedly reaching the area for Christ. Don himself also goes during February for a big meeting with all the local Christians, seeking to give a vision for the crusade. Then, when the Good News Crusade team eventually arrives, the ground is already prepared.

Don sees this preparation as a vital part of the whole crusade. He says, 'The evangelist doesn't produce souls. The local Christians are the ones who must reach the people. Only sheep can produce lambs. The evangelist is like a shepherd or a midwife. He preaches the Gospel and brings the people to the place of birth.

'This is an important principle when it comes to follow-up. When a sheep produces a lamb it will mother it. When people attend a crusade just through high-pressure advertising, they may come to Christ, but often drift back into the world. If brought to the meetings by Christians, whether family members, neighbours or workmates, a high percentage go on with the Lord.'

In late February, or early March, Mike Darwood goes ahead and for three days trains the counsellors. Not that Don or Mike advocate any technical 'know-how', for every soul is different. 'A soul should be led to Christ by the Spirit,' Don observes, 'but we do teach the prospective counsellors to pay attention to certain important points. We counsel them to look for a true repentance and to minister assurance. Also, in counselling there are many other things for which people need ministry.'

During the summer crusade, in addition to Don's regular team, he also recruits a temporary team of volunteers, many of them students, under the supervision of a mature leader. A special residential weekend is convened to give them some basic training.

With this sizable double-barrelled team, plus the enthusiastic co-operation of the local believers, things really begin to warm up as the Good News Crusade moves into a town.

Each morning David Abbott and Simon Matthews, each with their respective helpers, will be out visiting the local schools and addressing young people in their morning assemblies. Everyone else who is available meets together for a prayer session before fanning out to their various activities, which include door-knocking, coffee mornings in believers' houses (usually in several places each day), open-air witness, and in some cases visits to old people's homes, and jails.

During the morning Don dictates 'Good News Release' which a secretary stencils and duplicates ready for the evening meeting. This leaflet gives news of the previous day's happenings, some announcements, perhaps a new chorus to be used that night, or a book recommendation, and other matters of note.

At midday the whole team meets together for a united meal, prepared by the local catering unit. Most team members are accommodated in believers' homes for their sleeping quarters.

In the afternoon, Don and his team prepare for the evening meeting, while others engage in follow-up visits to those counselled the previous day. Some they catch around five or six o'clock on their return from work or school.

The children's meetings in the big tent begin at four-thirty; the youth meetings at six-thirty; and at seven o'clock Mike takes the 'school of faith' meetings. The latter is aimed at building up the faith of the believers in preparation for the main evangelistic service at 7.45, and usually has 'a terrific effect' on the meeting.

On Sunday morning, after a 9 a.m. prayer meeting, team members speak at local churches that are co-operating in the crusade. At 3 p.m. there is a family rally in the tent, and this meeting includes drama as a relevant way of communicating the message to this generation. Team members speak at local churches again in the evening and then there is the great after-church rally in the tent at night.

Don doesn't pray for the sick publicly every night. In this way, he deliberately avoids the possibility of building himself up as a cult figure. After a meeting, while the counsellors are busy with seekers, he will stand at the door of the main tent; shaking hands. If someone requests prayer for healing, he sends them to other members of the team. 'Today, I see evangelism very much as a body ministry, not as a one-man show,' he explains. The sick are therefore prayed for every night but not necessarily in the main meeting.

Counsellors are also taught to pray for people who want to be baptized in the Holy Spirit; and for those with deep hurts and embedded bitternesses; for marriage difficulties, and other problems; that God may heal them in the deepest recesses of their spirits.

The prayer tent is a hive of activity after each meeting. Every person counselled for salvation is given a Bible Study to complete, and introduced to a local church. The Bible Study Book currently used in the crusade is *Discipleship: The Daily Walk* by Mike Darwood.

The follow-up is planned and worked out in co-operation with the local churches, and the latest development has been the convening of a residential training weekend prior to the crusade season.

In 1978 basic follow-up teams, recruited from the churches in the areas where the crusades would be held, met with Mike and others of the team to discuss the problems of follow-up and to find solutions. Mike says, 'We gave some outlined plans for the year's follow-up.' These plans included the dividing up of the crusade areas into suitable districts, each with its own follow-up co-ordinator and team of workers, all under the direction of an overseer.

Mike pinpoints the aim of follow-up as being:

(a) To establish the convert's personal relationship with the Lord through prayer and Bible study.

(b) To allocate a personal counsellor to each convert who will be responsible for follow-up for at least three months.

(c) To organize mid-week discipleship groups of 8-12 converts, with a leader and assistant.

(d) To get the converts established in the fellowship of a local church.

In the two years since these plans have been put into operation, the percentage of converts still going on with

141

the Lord after a year or more, and still attending house meetings has jumped from an estimated 10 or 15% (which is as much as anyone usually claims) to about 50%. But Don and the team are not satisfied with this and are 'believing God that with more efficiency we shall be able to keep more in the net'.

In the months following a crusade, three post-crusade rallies are held, and then Don conducts a final rally towards the close of the year. Mike, Simon, David and Robert Parkinson also all make return visits until the local churches are fully equipped to carry on with the work of training new converts.

As each year has brought more and more demands for ministry, Don has learnt the hard way that rest and refreshment are intended to be part of the Lord's programme.

An extra crusade in 1978 crowded out his scheduled holiday and by the end of the year he was totally exhausted. The only answer was a month's 'sabbatical'. Mike Darwood, also in need of a break, joined him for this. They spent the mornings with the Bible, taking 'The Kingdom of God' as their theme of study. Then a midday walk followed by relaxation with the family completed their day. Don returned to work at the end of the time healed and refreshed.

From time to time, when his busy schedule allows, Don appreciates the opportunity to sit under the ministry of other men and women of God.

He is also a very willing participant in any united witness to the nation, whether as an invited speaker, or merely as a supporter.

At the Trafalgar Square Festival of Light in 1971, Don found himself in a most unexpected role. While standing in the crowd listening to one of the speakers, he became aware of a sudden stir behind him. A weirdly dressed fellow came pushing through the throng, obviously making a bee-line for the platform.

'I'm Jesus Christ. Excuse me. Let Jesus Christ come by. I'm the Son of God. I'm Jesus Christ. Let me through,' demanded the man as he jostled his way along. 'And,' says Don incredulously, 'people were standing aside and making way for him!'

As the man approached from behind, Don deliberately turned and put his hand on his shoulder. 'Excuse me sir,' he began politely, 'but who did you say you were?'

'I'm the Lord Jesus Christ, the Son of God,' the poor fellow repeated grandly.

'Well, I'm very sorry,' Don contradicted gently, 'you couldn't possibly be Him you know, because He's in here,' pointing to his heart.

With that, the demented man turned meekly and walked quietly away, and Don, relieved, felt more than glad that he had been on the spot to save the gathering from an unpleasant disturbance.

One of the greatest secrets of Don's successful ministry across the years has been the sustained emphasis on believing prayer. Besides regular prayer for the work, a day of prayer and fasting always precedes the crusade season and the Easter Convention. A confidential prayer fellowship letter also calls Don's many friends to stand with them in intercession in all their many endeavours. Deeply conscious of his need of the power of the Holy Spirit, and of his dependence on the prayers of God's people, Don never likes to hear people praising his ministry.

'Don't talk to people about us,' he tells his admirers, 'talk to them about Jesus.' 'But,' he twinkles characteristically, 'when you are talking to the Lord Jesus, then—talk about us.'

21

God Pays for What He Orders

Every Christian enterprise must have its financial policy, and the Good News Crusade is no exception. But like many another work of faith, its only guaranteed sponsor has always been the Lord Himself. Even the rapid increase in the scope of the work in recent years has not shaken Don's confidence and that of his co-workers, that 'God pays for what He orders'.

Each member of the team lives by faith and receives no salary. General funds pay for the overheads of the work, but each individual on the team is responsible for praying in his own keep and that of his family. There is no pooling. Each worker has his own living quarters and looks after his own finances, but all are deeply committed to one another. 'Everyone is thrilled with the arrangement,' says Don, 'and wouldn't wish to have it any other way.'

Not that it is always easy. There have been times when a team member has felt obliged to take on a part time job in order to make ends meet. But these occasions have been the exception rather than the rule.

'But,' you may ask, 'what about the girls in the office and families in administrative and bookshop work?' 'Do they get as well cared for as the members of the team who are out preaching regularly?'

Don recognizes this difference and replies, 'It is our policy that those in the limelight seek to be sensitive to the needs of others in the team, and minister to them from what God gives us.'

At Don's main evangelistic crusades the only offering taken up publically is a thank-offering on the last night, which is given in full to overseas missionary work. Expenses for the crusade in any given area are prayed in locally, and a box for free-will offering is left at the door for this purpose.

The main reason for refraining from taking a public offering on these occasions is the large number of unconverted people who are usually present. But on other occasions when Christians would be in the majority, the offering is a regular part of the worship.

At the Ipswich Convention once a year, a love-offering is taken at every service, each being designated for the various team members and for the invited guest speakers.

With regard to public appeals and making the needs of the work known, Don believes that, as in other matters, it is all important to listen to the voice of the Holy Spirit.

To illustrate this principle Don relates the way in which God provided them with a new projector some years ago.

'We had an old Italian thing that kept breaking down,' he recalls. 'At that time we were reaching many souls for Christ with films, and felt it right to step out and buy a new projector, in faith that the money would be provided. We took delivery, and the same night had a film rally. About two hundred and fifty people were present. As I was about to announce the offering I thought I would just say a word about the need to pay for the projector.

'I opened my mouth, but at that moment the Lord spoke to me very clearly, "Don't you dare mention it." I obeyed and said nothing. Later on while shaking hands at the door, a lady pressed a bundle into my hands. When I looked and counted it (for it was a bundle of five-pound notes) I found that it amounted to two hundred pounds. This together with the allowance on the old projector, taken in part exchange, fully paid for the new one.'

Don adds, 'This is a principle I have found working right through my ministry. On some issues the Lord makes it clear that I am not allowed to mention the need publicly, but just to pray about it. At other times I feel He leads me to make a need known and to encourage the members of the body of Christ to pray with us and to give.'

Some very large items, such as the Hammond Organ, were fully provided through prayer alone. But the Good News Crusade is not in bondage over this matter one way or the other. They believe that true prayer partners will want to know the facts and help to bear the burden. 'The important thing is to be led by the Spirit in each situation,' Don emphasizes. This openness of mind has led Don into some unusual experiences in the realm of finance, like the time when God instructed him to borrow money on behalf of a Christian friend in serious trouble. Involved in some complicated business deals, this friend, with no evil intent, found himself outside of the law. Now he stood trial accused of embezzlement, facing a possible three-year sentence.

The night before the final hearing Don and Heather stayed at his home, virtually the only friends still standing with him and his wife through the crisis. They talked and prayed and agonized together about the situation until nearly midnight.

'You know, if I had the money, I'd do something and clear this. But there's nothing I can do,' Don mused sadly. At this juncture, the wife left the room weeping, and went upstairs to bed. While her footsteps were still sounding on the stairs, Don heard the voice of the Lord, as he expresses it, 'clear as a bell'. 'There is something you can do.' 'What Lord? What can I do?' Don pleaded eagerly. 'There is someone from whom you can borrow the money,' the Lord told him, bringing to his mind the name of a certain Christian man.

With scarcely a second thought, Don left the house and made his way quickly to a public phone box, putting through a call to the person God had indicated. This fine brother responded immediately, writing out a cheque and arranging for its speedy delivery.

Next day in court, Don presented the cheque and spoke in favour of his friend, telling of the tremendous blessing and influence for good he had been in his own life as a young man, and virtually gave a potted testimony.

This testimonial, together with the covering finance, influenced the decision of the court to the extent that they handed down a very short sentence. How God over-ruled the whole affair and brought good out of it for Don's friend is another fascinating story, one that does not belong within the scope of this narrative.

Don's attitude to money is relaxed and optimistic. He likes to say, 'There is no inflation in heaven.'

Several years ago when Harold Wilson was Prime Minister, an afternoon radio music programme paused for a special announcement. Regretfully Mr Wilson informed his listeners of a six-pence increase in petrol prices. 'Hallelujah,' shouted Don exuberantly. 'Darling,' he continued, as his wife looked at him mildly. 'Isn't it wonderful? We're going to have to trust Jesus for another six-pence for every twenty-five miles we travel. We're going to have to use our faith again!'

But Don is human and there are times when his faith needs an extra boost.

While negotiating the purchase of a larger house in

1976 he learnt from an acquaintance that solicitors' fees were likely to be far in excess of his own estimation. Staggered at the figure mentioned, his faith took a sharp nose-dive.

That weekend saw a Teens' and Twenties' Conference, and Don ministered to the young people on the gifts of the Holy Spirit, with particular emphasis on how to prophesy, encouraging them to step out in faith. Not long afterwards during one of the meetings where the Holy Spirit was moving in power, a young girl timidly gave her first ever word of prophecy. Knowing nothing of the problem with which Don was grappling, she stood to her feet and made the proclamation, 'Thus says the Lord, 'I want you to know that I am not about to go bankrupt.''' With that she sat down hurriedly.

Don knew immediately that the message was for him and his faith shot right back up to its usual level. God had used a seemingly insignificant teenager to be His messenger and to encourage His servant on this occasion.

In matters of finance the Good News Crusade is very conscious of the interdependence of the members of the body of Christ. Once while Don was away in Africa his little son Joel asked Heather for a banana. There were none in the house at the time and Heather had already spent her last penny. 'We'll have to pray and ask Jesus to send us some money,' she told him. Next day some funds arrived in the post. Heather went out and bought the bananas telling Joel that Jesus had supplied the pennies. The little boy thought deeply for a moment and then demanded innocently, 'How did He send them? Did He throw them out of the sky?' This gave Heather the opportunity to explain to her little boy what many of God's older children often fail to realize—that God certainly does not throw money out of the sky.

The Bible teaches that 'The Lord ordained that they

148

which preach the gospel should live of the gospel' (1 Corinthians 9:14). Unless those to whom God has entrusted regular wages, or even wealth, realize this principle, and share with those in full-time ministry, some of God's faithful servants from time to time must experience areas of want. Answers to prayer in most cases have to come through Christians who are sensitive to the voice of the Holy Spirit telling them when and where to minister, when and where to give.

22

Don the Family Man

Travelling in distant lands on the Lord's business, be it in Africa, Japan, or anywhere else on earth, Don always has a weather-eye open for the postman; for he is never far away in spirit from the family he has to leave behind on these occasions.

Don is basically a home-loving man and enjoys to the full the brief periods he is able to spend with Heather and the children.

These are times for feeding the ducks in the park; for bringing out the beautiful animal photographs that Don himself snapped for the children while in Africa; and for exchanging the dignity of the pulpit for romps on the living room floor, where Joel and Faith take turns for pony rides on his back.

Don also likes to put in a bit of gardening, reminiscent of his farming days, and enjoys cooking, especially trying out new recipes.

Christmas is always reserved as a family time when Don aims to be home for ten days or more. Invariably he cooks hamburgers on Christmas Eve and likes to help Heather pack the Christmas stockings.

These happy family occasions provide excellent opportunities for reminiscing and bringing out ageless stories . . . like the one about the time when Don was in the army stationed at Fleet.

Don couldn't swim, so they took him along to the

local swimming pool to teach him, and pushed him, tall as he was, in at the deep end. For a breathless second Don struggled and spluttered, then suddenly his face appeared above the water. No, he wasn't swimming. He was standing up! Incidentally, he never did learn to swim.

Another tale that never fails to produce gales of laughter is the one about the time the family visited friends on a farm. These friends owned a lovely pony and everybody had to have a turn at riding it bare-back, hanging on to its mane.

The pony behaved beautifully until it came to Don's turn. Then the canny beast apparently decided that a two-hundred pound evangelist whose legs almost touched the ground was just too much of a good thing. She refused to budge.

Eventually, after much cajoling and prodding, she bolted. But the pony, instead of heading up the paddock, dashed towards a nearby barn, losing her burden as she charged through the low door. Don saved his head by grabbing hold of the lintel of the door, and was left dangling briefly, to the everlasting amusement of the beholders.

Don and Heather's lively household quite often turns into an 'extended family', as frequently one or more of the younger team members will live in with them, not to mention other guests who drop in from time to time. But Don and Heather look upon their home as the Lord's, and right from the time God gave them a place of their own, they have adopted the attitude, 'Lord, you can send whoever you like here, just as long as you keep the pantry full.'

In addition to the pleasure of returning home to Heather and the children in Cornwall, Don also looks forward to the times when they are all able to visit his parents, who still live in Hadleigh, near Ipswich. On these occasions he can hardly get there fast enough. 'And we know when he's here,' beams his mother, 'because he's always singing.'

The Double's two older children, now married, both have high praise for their father. Although he spent the greater part of the time away, they never felt neglected or uncared for.

Julia recalls, 'My earliest memories of my father are of his goings and comings. Although they brought disappointment and joy respectively, they were not hardships.

'I can remember getting very excited for several days before Dad came home. He usually brought us something as a gift, which of course added to the excitement. Dad always came home at Christmas and was also with us on my birthday in August, as we were usually on holiday with him at that time. We looked forward to these occasions in anticipation of having great fun and lots of "treats"!

'One of the first Christmases I can recall was when I was about six. I remember Nigel and me getting into the big double bed with Dad at approximately 6 a.m. to open our presents. Dad was always very generous towards us and if he got to know that we wanted something special, he always tried his utmost to get it for us.

'Easter too was always a very special time of the year, as not only did Dad come home but there was also the Easter Convention. I can't remember Easter without the Convention.'

With regard to discipline Don's daughter continues, 'In our family relationships I have always looked upon Dad as a person who knows the right time for discipline. I wouldn't say he was strict, but neither would I say that he was free-and-easy. He was, and still is, a person who looks at both motives and actions.

'I remember when I was about eight years old, on one

occasion we had a little battle. I had a peach stone in my mouth and refused to spit it out. Dad sent me to my room and made me stay there until I did spit it out. He knew it would be no good spanking me. The best way to cure that kind of stubbornness was for me to punish myself.

'One of the things I have really come to value has been Dad's prayers for me. I know he still prays for us every day, and that is a great source of strength to me. During the time I was taking my "O" levels at school I can remember saying to Dad every morning, "Don't forget to pray for me." During the exam itself I would feel a sudden burst of anointing and think to myself, "How good it is to have Dad praying for me."

'I still feel and appreciate his prayers, as he is the one who first senses when something is wrong with me. The times are few and far between when he doesn't know how my relationship stands with the Lord. At times I have regretted the fact that I can't seem to hide anything from Dad, but deep down I have known it to be very valuable to me, and I am thankful.'

Son Nigel adds, 'As a father I have always found him to be God's man of the moment, ready with encouragement or when necessary, discouragement, for the things which crop up in a young person's life.

'I was pointed in the right direction and if I stopped or slipped back I knew that he knew. Then he either gave me a gentle push to start me off again, or sometimes just the fact that I knew he knew would start me off again. I would say that my father has been the biggest influence of all others in my own ministry.'

The close relationship between Don and his son as a teenager proved to be the final deciding factor in the conversion of a Canadian woman.

While in England for a visit, this woman was taken by friends to a convention where Don was one of the speakers. All week long she listened to inspirational messages from one and another, but her will remained untouched.

On the last day, Nigel arrived. Don on the look-out for him greeted him in the foyer, and throwing his arms around his son, they kissed each other. The Canadian lady standing nearby observed this display of affection, and found herself deeply moved. That night she gave her heart to the Lord.

She told Don later, 'Mr Double, when I saw how much you and your teenage son loved each other, it moved me more than all the messages I had heard.'

In a decadent age when there is no real rapport between parents and their children, the love of Christ had been seen as a reality and not just as a subject-matter for sermons.

With regard to the training of children in the things of the Lord, Don says, 'I will not allow my children to lean on my experience of God, but from the earliest age teach them to prove Him for themselves.'

One example of how this works out is seen in the case of Stephen who, although still a child, has learnt to give to God beyond his means. In his eleventh year he gave £40 to the work of the Lord, all of which God had provided outside of his regular pocket money.

The following New Year at the annual conference, he put a faith promise for £30 into the offering and within 24 hours had received a £60 cheque. The following Easter, he put in a promise amounting to £40. Shortly afterwards someone at the Easter Convention handed him a cheque for £50.

'Now,' says Don, 'If they had given those cheques to me, I could easily understand it. But people don't give cheques like that to eleven or twelve-year-old boys. It's just not done. And incidentally, those cheques were not given by people that know Stephen or us very well—

154

just by visitors to the conferences and conventions. It proves that God is faithful to His Word. When we give to Him, He gives to us, pressed down, shaken together, and running over.'

Don has sometimes been criticized for leaving his family, especially when, as on the occasion of his visit to Japan in 1973, a new baby had only recently arrived. But Heather and the rest of the family have an understanding about these things, and he goes with their blessing.

Julia sums up the feelings of them all by saying, 'I don't think I could have a better father. I don't say this at all lightly but realistically. Our family is right behind him as a person and as a ministry. I know that I for one thank God for the privilege of being a part of him.'

23

'A Time to Heal...'

Ecclesiastes 3:3

In the ministry of the Good News Crusade, the message of healing has always gone hand in hand with the message of salvation. Don believes that the will of God embraces physical healing and that our part is to reach out in faith to receive His touch of power. He also believes that no malady is too small or too great to merit God's attention, and the variety of miracles recorded over the years bear witness to this fact.

A sample taken from the records at random includes the healing of insomnia, hernia, fractured pelvis, blindness, deafness, paralysis, gall stones, disseminated sclerosis, rheumatoid arthritis, rheumatism, migraine, cancer, deformities, asthma, angina, sugar diabetes; not to mention deliverances from alcoholism, drug addiction, and habits such as nail-biting and smoking; and countless other infirmities.

If pressed to give details about individuals who have been healed during any particular period, Don usually shakes his head regretfully and replies, 'I'm sorry, but I never had a good memory for miracles. Within a week or two I usually forget them. I think one of the reasons is that God graciously causes so much to happen in our ministry that what is taking place currently is enough for anyone to remember.'

Happily, a few of the outstanding cases have been documented, and testimonies continually flow in to the

St Austell office by phone or letter, telling of the wonderful things God has done and is doing.

Mrs Nellie Wallis is a lady in her sixties who attends most of Don's crusades and glowingly testifies to the great miracle God did in her life.

Don first met Mrs Wallis during two nights of special evangelism in a Baptist Church, arranged by a young man who had been converted at one of Don's tent meetings.

Mrs Wallis attended the first service wearing a heavy spinal collar. Explaining her condition at that time she testifies, 'The bones at the top of my spine had deteriorated. My right hand was swollen and bent and if anyone accidentally touched it, I fainted with the pain. An ambulance took me to the hospital for treatment three times a week.'

That first night there were no miracles. The sick had never been prayed for in that church before and Don felt it wise to tread carefully. However, he did mention healing in his message and spoke with such conviction that Mrs Wallis found herself reacting rather negatively.

After the service she approached Don and challenged him, 'Don't you think that pain is something we have to bear as part of our testimony to the world?'

'Show me where it says that in the Bible,' Don replied bluntly, though not unkindly.

'I didn't take to him at all,' Nellie says apologetically, recalling her first prejudiced impressions. 'I felt repulsed and didn't want to go again.'

Next day, looking for a good excuse to stay away, Nellie phoned her daughter. 'How about you going to the meeting tonight? I'll baby-sit for you,' she offered.

'No, mother. I think you ought to go,' her daughter told her firmly. Reluctantly she complied.

That second evening as Don spoke, Nellie experienced an inward battle. 'I was too troubled to really know

157

what he said,' she recalls, 'then suddenly, peace came. When Don made the appeal I knew I must go forward and that I would be healed.'

Nellie rose to her feet and together with about six other people made her way to the front of the church.

Don lined up the people and began to pray for them one by one. As he reached Mrs Wallis and laid his hands on her, he felt the power of God go through her, and knew that something had happened. He moved on to the next person and bowed his head. As Don was about to pray he became aware of a crunching sound behind him. Looking around, he saw Mrs Wallis tearing off her neck brace.

'It was quite a shocking experience for me in that Baptist Church,' Don recollects, 'and the congregation began to get very excited because of course they knew her.'

Taking up the story Mrs Wallis explains her action. 'As soon as Don prayed for me I felt my shoulders drop. They had previously been in a fixed position, and as they dropped I felt the Lord saying, "You're healed. You don't need that collar now!" So I took it off.'

Nellie unlatched the collar and held it in her right hand which had previously been useless. Minutes later when someone excitedly came over and reached to shake her hand, her husband winced, unconsciously expecting some cry of pain. But no cry came. Joyfully, she returned the handshake.

That night in her own home, Nellie rediscovered a pleasure that had long been denied her. She could use soap again to wash her hands!

Three days later Nellie Wallis kept her Friday appointment at the hospital. This was her day to see the specialist.

'Well, how are you?' he queried without looking up from his desk as she entered the room.

'I'm all right. There's nothing the matter now. I've been healed,' she replied matter of factly.

'Umm, well, we'll soon see about that,' the specialist condescended in his best humouring tone, as he rose to his feet.

Nellie chuckles delightedly as she recounts how he twisted her neck backwards and forwards.

'This can't be,' he frowned in a puzzled manner, giving it another twist. 'Now when do you come back for your next treatment? I don't quite know what to do. Let's see. You're due to see me again in one month. Shall we make it six weeks?'

Nellie went back six weeks later but did not see the usual specialist. Another doctor attended her.

'I'm going to discharge you,' he told her. 'However, the X-ray shows that there is still some deterioration in the bones. I'm afraid you'll be back before long, and you'll just have to learn to live with it.'

'But that was more than six years ago. And I'm still fine. My general health is good too,' Nellie Wallis testifies happily.

Another healing testimony comes from Dr Adjie of Ghana. Throughout his years in medical school Dr Adjie suffered from abdominal discomfort. For a while he successfully ignored the trouble, but after he qualified the pain became worse, being especially bad in the early morning.

Investigations by a general practitioner revealed nothing tangible, so Dr Adjie was referred to two specialists. Examinations, barium meals, and X-rays all resulted in no clear cut diagnosis. Medicine brought no relief. The pain persisted.

Following this, Dr Adjie, who was already a Christian, attended a Don Double crusade in Ampthill, Bedfordshire, taking some of his patients with him.

He describes the meetings as 'Thrilling! Tremendous!' He went most nights and witnessed a number of healings. But it never occurred to him to seek healing for himself.

One evening after Don had finished speaking and had given the invitation, and a number had moved out to the prayer tent for counselling, suddenly Don received a word of knowledge from the Lord.

He indicated that there was someone present with a specific problem needing help in a specific way. He then began to elaborate, and pinpointed the need as an abdominal condition, one which the medical profession had been unable to diagnose.

At this point Dr Adjie recognized that the Lord was singling him out, so he stood to his feet and made his need known.

Don called him to the front, prayed for him and the pain left immediately. But next morning would be the real test. The pain was usually severe and persistent from three, four, or five o'clock, continuing until he got up and walked about. But next morning Dr Adjie experienced no discomfort at all. The condition, whatever it had been, had cleared up completely.

The testimony of Mrs Diana Wright of Ipswich concerning the healing of a knee infection following an operation for cancer is best told in her own words.

'My left knee had been hurting for about two years and had been diagnosed as arthritis. However, in the autumn of 1974 it began to give way beneath me as I walked, and I went for an X-ray. . . . They found a tumour in the bone of the knee and in five days I was in Ipswich Hospital. The consultant there did a biopsy, but then explained that it was worse than he had feared and referred me to the top bone specialist in the country —Mr D. R. Sweetnam, F.R.C.A., Consultant Orthopaedic Surgeon at the Middlesex Hospital. I was then just twenty-nine.'

'The biopsy report said that cancer could not be confirmed but must be suspected. After second and third
opinions Mr Sweetnam decided that they had caught it
just in time, dug it all out and packed it with bone chips
taken from my right hip. I was then on crutches for
three months—with three children, the baby being just
nine months old. But the presence of Jesus' and His
peace was with me and our family through it all . . . .'

'It looked as if all was well after the operation, but
infection set in and the wound just would not heal and
kept discharging. The doctors tried every antibiotic
both orally and by injection with no improvement. Then
they took me in for a month on a "drip" pouring in
massive amounts of antibiotics day and night.

'It was on the Wednesday before Easter 1975 that Mr
Sweetnam came and announced that he would have to
operate again and possibly amputate the leg. He said,
"You can either go home for Easter and return on
Monday for operation Wednesday, or stay and I'll do it
tomorrow."'

'What a choice! I wanted to go home and see my
family. But where would I find the courage to return on
Monday? I said, "Do it tomorrow." But I phoned my
husband and he said, "Come home." Mr Sweetnam
agreed with my husband, so it was two against one, and
it proved to be in the plan of God.

'We came to the Good News Crusade Easter Convention on the Friday. Then on the Sunday night we planned
to go again, but I had a lot of ironing and packing for the
children to go to their Grandma's and Satan tried to stop
us going. We eventually arrived there late.

'The meeting was practically over when Don had a
word of knowledge from God about three people there
with back trouble, and they went forward for prayer.
Then he said, "There is someone here tonight with a
bad knee—the left knee."

'I said, "Yes, that's me. I'm due to go into hospital tomorrow for another operation." Don prayed for me, and then Mike Darwood said, "The Lord tells you the infection is healed."

'I clung to those words as I went back into hospital the next day. And I told the houseman, who told the registrar, who told the consultant, who came running and said, "I hear there is a new dimension in this case!"

'I told Mr Sweetnam what had happened and the registrar said, "Was he your local vicar?" So I said, "No. They came from Cornwall. They could not have known anything about me. It could only have been God speaking." Then the registrar said, "Well, it doesn't look healed, does it?" and I had to agree with him. But I said, "Maybe God is waiting to see if I really believe it is going to heal." Mr Sweetnam then said, "Well, God can do what He likes. If He says it's healed, you'd better go home." Thus it was exactly twenty-four hours after I went in that I came home again.

'Within two weeks the wound had completely dried up and healed perfectly. When I went back, Mr Sweetnam was nearly as delighted as I was and proceeded to tell all his students: "You remember Mrs Wright? Well, that's the knee the Almighty healed." He even sent the sister to find the unbelieving registrar "to see what God has done . . ." and he was the only person who was "not too happy."'

For two years Mrs Wright led a normal life, even playing tennis, but continued to go for check-ups every few months. A further tumour and another operation in March 1977, far from detracting from the wonder of the former healing, provided her with an opportunity to share her experience with a group of American Consultants visiting for a conference.

Continuing her story Diana Wright says, 'Mr Sweetnam told them of my previous history and of the infection that had plagued me for six months. "But that healed rather dramatically," he said, and proceeded to invite me to tell them how the Lord had spoken saying, "The infection is healed." What a thrill that was to be able to testify to these top men that Jesus still heals today. I knew of a certainty that I was in His place for me and that He was taking me through that operation. . . . We had no trouble with infection this time and . . . within a month I was home.'

Another interesting report comes from a Church of England minister, the Rev. Frank L. Thomas. Don in the pulpit does not always know all that goes on in a congregation during his meetings. Frank Thomas wrote to him in November 1976 following a weekend of renewal when Don and Heather had ministered in his church at Lowestoft in Suffolk. 'On the Sunday night the power of the Lord was present to heal. One lady who had been in a car crash previously which did permanent injury to a knee joint was wonderfully healed during the singing of "By His stripes we are healed". So too was a woman with no sense of touch in her extremities. She received sensitivity and feeling and warmth in hands and feet (and she was to sleep her first night in years without any pain). Both of these people I have seen since and they are still rejoicing in the Lord. There were others too, all in one area of the congregation. The singing of angels was also heard by a number of people in that part of the church. I have met several who quite independently witnessed to this. . . .'

In the same church, a lady who received healing for deafness also had a baby sick in hospital. Don told her in the Spirit that the baby would be home and well by the end of the week. By Tuesday the baby had improved so much that the doctor looked at him and said, 'What's that child doing here?' and sent him home the same day.

A beautiful story of healing comes from a lady in

Northamptonshire, and illustrates how God moves through the whole team during the crusades.

The lady in question had been ill for many years, and in 1968 her condition was diagnosed as manic depressive psychosis, thought to be due to a chemical imbalance following the birth of her daughter.

'It is difficult to describe the utter despair I felt as the depressions became very severe,' she writes. 'To make matters worse my husband did not believe I was ill and said that I "put it on".

'It was difficult to face the days. Really indescribable. However, I received a drug which had to be monitored in my blood . . . I had to have regular blood tests, weekly to begin with.'

Years later, divorced, and still on medication, Mrs X heard that the GNC were coming to the area. The occasion was the June 1977 Nene Valley Crusade, and she attended with a quiet expectation that healing (in spite of the specialist's 'no cure' pronouncement) lay within the realm of possibility, for 'with God all things are possible'.

She takes up the tale: 'The first evening I attended, I was enveloped in the warmth and Christian love of the service. At the end, I slipped away from my friends and entered the prayer tent.

'A sister (one of the temporary team) came towards me and took my arm. For the first time, I was able to condense the details of my illness, and tell her the despair I felt. She called another lady over and they laid hands on me and prayed and spoke in tongues. The tears rolled down my face, flowing like a river, and I felt a deep peace.'

When at the Saturday service Don asked for those who had received healing to stand and declare it, Mrs X stood and before nine hundred people bore testimony to what God had done. She also visited her doctor and with face aglow told him her story. The doctor, who in the past had always warned her not to leave off her tablets, replied, 'I can see you are healed. There is no need for the tablets any more.'

The healing which took place at this time was deep and lasting. 'What joy!' she writes. 'Each morning I awoke ready and happy to face the day. Everyone saw the change in me. I was full of praise that our Lord had blessed me. The sister and the other lady at my healing visited me at home, and the fellowship we had was wonderful. We met again at this year's crusade (1979).'

Don himself has had a number of personal experiences of divine healing, besides the occasion of the healing of the anal fissure soon after his conversion.

In 1970 Don was holding a crusade at Godmanchester and stayed in the home of Mike and Muriel Darwood prior to their joining the team.

Don had been troubled by a painful hip for about eighteen months, which he took to be arthritis, and it was growing progressively worse. He couldn't stand for long and had to preach with his knee resting on a shelf inside the pulpit.

Describing his predicament, he wrote in *Ripened Grain* in 1971, 'I was praying for the sick and seeing God heal them, but I could not accept the miracle I needed for myself.'

At this time Jean Darnall came to Ampthill to hold meetings, and Don took his team over for an afternoon to support Jean and also to receive a little spiritual refreshment for themselves. Don says, 'Jean knew absolutely nothing about my hip and we didn't get to greet each other before the meeting started.'

Towards the close of the service, when Jean began to pray for the sick, she invited Don up on to the platform to help her. As she turned to pray for someone, Don hobbled out, and hardly knowing how to stand, prayed for one and another of those waiting their turn. He then returned to his seat in the congregation.

Meanwhile, Jean had received a word of knowledge from the Lord. She straightened up and announced in clear tones, 'There is someone here with a severe pain in the right hip.'

All Don's team turned and pointed at him. 'No wonder I felt it so strongly when standing near you,' Jean commented, as Don hobbled out again.

Jean prayed for Don, but as he returned to Godmanchester that afternoon the pain grew worse than ever. Still determined to continue with his own crusade, Don prepared for the evening meeting, then left the house and started on his way. Suddenly the pain left him and he knew that God had touched him. Don has had no further trouble with his hip since. His healing was complete.

Don experienced yet another healing in 1973. Before he was twenty he developed varicose veins, the condition being hereditary on his father's side. Don believes that serving point duty as a Regimental Policeman brought the trouble on earlier than might otherwise have been expected.

In 1973 the varicose veins on one leg broke out into a huge ulcer about six inches by three inches, during the Blaithwaite Camp.

He was in terrible pain and could hardly walk. So as soon as he returned home, he went to see his local doctor who dressed the leg and told him to go to bed. He also promised to get a specialist in to look at it as soon as possible, so that Don could go straight into hospital.

Don arrived home and went to bed. As he lay there thinking, he realized with a jolt that within a few days he must start a new crusade at Silsby, near Leicester. Ten thousand hand bills as well as posters had already gone out. He was also booked to speak on the BBC

Radio Programme *Thought for the Day* for a whole week.

This was no time for being sick or going into hospital. 'Lord, what am I doing lying here?' he pleaded. Then he prayed: 'Lord, unless it's your will for me to be here, that specialist can't get near this house. I believe you to keep him away.'

Hour after hour passed away. No specialist arrived. About nine o'clock that evening the family doctor turned up and apologised. 'Mr Double, the telephone lines to the specialist have been jammed all day long. I've just not been able to contact him.'

'Good,' thought Don. Aloud he said, 'Dr Phillips, I'm going to Silsby on Tuesday.'

'You're what?' asked the doctor.

'I'm going to Silsby on Tuesday.'

'You can't.'

'I'm going.'

'Look, if you go your leg will get worse. They'll probably have to put you in hospital up there. You've no choice.'

'Well, I'm going anyway.'

Dr Phillips could see that Don was determined and gave in reluctantly. 'I'll get the nurse round to clean up your leg and strap it up,' he promised. 'If you must go, you must, but it's your responsibility.'

The nurse soon came round, and being a God-fearing woman supported Don's decision.

Don couldn't drive the two hundred and fifty miles to Silsby in his condition, so Heather drove instead, and the first night of the crusade he stood and preached in terrible pain.

The second night while preaching Don felt the touch of the Lord upon him. His leg improved rapidly from that moment, and within a day or two there were no ill effects at all.

Don continued in the crusade as planned for sixteen days and then returned home.

The nurse arrived soon after, stripped off the strappings on Don's leg and found the ulcer completely healed. 'That's a miracle,' she marvelled.

After the nurse had reported back to Doctor Phillips he phoned Don. 'Will you please come down to the surgery and show me your miracle.' When he saw it he acknowledged, 'I must admit that prayer has helped to heal that.'

Don's doctor has a hearty respect for Don's ministry, and during one of their many chats together told him, 'Mr Double, you can do more to help fifty per cent of the people that come into my surgery than I can. So many of their troubles stem from the fact that they have nothing to believe in.'

Don feels concerning his own physical needs such as the painful hip and the ulcerated leg that God allowed him to experience them in order to teach him compassion and understanding for others who suffer pain.

In 1977 Don was scheduled to go to Chile for evangelistic ministry, together with Mike Darwood. The preceding week Don had a full programme of meetings, appointments and administrative work and felt quite exhausted. It seemed he would get no time to relax or even pack his case.

On the Tuesday evening, prior to their departure the following Monday, a small bone lodged itself in Don's throat as he ate some fish.

It didn't actually hurt, but was troublesome enough for him to be aware of its presence. Special prayer brought no relief, so by Thursday Don decided to consult his doctor.

The doctor immediately sent him to the hospital where they removed the bone under a general anaesthetic.

Don took one and a half hours to come out of the anaesthetic and had to stay in the hospital until midday on the Friday and rest for the whole weekend.

Don's own commentary on these events acknowledges the sovereignty of God in His dealings with us. 'The Lord sometimes permits in His wisdom what He could prevent with His power.' Don knew that he desperately needed that break, and confesses that the enforced rest became an invaluable contribution to the subsequent ministry in Chile.

24

Chile

'Chile is a great country. I never enjoyed ministering in any country so much in my life,' Don wrote after his visit there in October 1977.

The call to Chile came through Alf Cooper, a young missionary of the South American Missionary Society. He is also a member of the Par Gospel Church.

Alf had returned to the land of his birth as a missionary and, having secured a warm invitation for Don and Mike from the Anglican churches with which he is associated, eagerly awaited the visit of his friends.

Following the episode with the fish bone, Don and Mike packed their bags, said their good-byes, and set out for Heathrow Airport. 'I wonder what Chile will really be like,' Don pondered, recalling the various newspaper reports he had read concerning repression and governmental heavy-handedness in that country. 'I wonder how we'll be received and how it will all work out.'

But such musings were brought to an abrupt end when they reached Heathrow, for more immediate problems confronted them. The airport traffic was at a standstill. Frustrated passengers milled around everywhere, asking questions and looking for some action.

First, there had been an early morning fog. Then the air-controllers had gone on strike. What next? Then things were just beginning to get back to normal and

Don and Mike about to board their plane with the KLM baggage handlers decided it was their turn. Another strike!

Already late evening, Don and Mike had no alternative other than to accept the hotel accommodation provided by KLM for their disappointed clients; and since the hotel restaurant had already closed for the night, the weary would-be travellers went hungry to bed.

The following evening after another tiring day of hanging about, they finally left from Gatwick at about 9 p.m. having changed both airlines and airports. They now winged their way towards the new experiences awaiting them in the Republic of Chile.

Approximately eighteen hours later, the men arrived in Santiago, Chile's capital. Bathed in afternoon sunshine, the city seemed to smile a welcome, the clear blue skies showing off to perfection the magnificent snow-capped peaks of the Andes Mountains, which form the backdrop of the local scenery.

Alf was on hand to greet the visitors, together with a local Anglican bishop, both in high spirits and excited at the prospect of Don and Mike's three-week-long ministry among them.

The bishop's mini-bus soon whisked them away to the home of an Anglo-Chilean Christian. There they were greeted by the Spanish-speaking housekeeper, with smiles and plenty of good food. And in spite of the delay in arrival they still had time to stretch out on their beds for a short rest before being plunged into the busy round of ministry.

They started off that night with a question-and-answer meeting for church leaders. There were pastors, elders, and leaders of house groups, from various parts of the city. Some were from churches already experiencing renewal. Others came asking questions and voicing concern over some emphases which had brought the movement into disrepute in their eyes.

Alf, who interpreted for Don and Mike throughout the whole tour, wrote afterwards, 'God gave such wisdom, and wit, that about forty leaders who had never met before caught the vision for the future of renewal in Santiago.'

The next few days were packed full with meetings in different churches, several described as 'unforgettable'. One of these was a service in the English Community Church. Catering to the English-speaking population in an otherwise Spanish community, this church embraces business people, British Embassy staff, and various others of western culture, who speak only broken English.

The subject for the evening, healing, quickened faith and laid the foundation for a moving of the Spirit of God, which caused the vicar to exclaim, 'This church has never seen anything like this before.'

Another outstanding gathering took place at a week-night meeting in a charismatic Roman Catholic Church in the suburbs. Don wrote, 'The place was jammed to capacity, about four hundred being present; the biggest attendance they had ever known. . . . The people took off in worship of the Lord in beautiful freedom, the gifts flowing as they functioned as the body of Christ. I preached the word of God uncompromisingly, and at the end about one hundred and fifty responded, receiving Jesus Christ as their personal Saviour and Lord.'

Perhaps one of the most exciting occasions for Don and Mike was when they preached at the huge Methodist Pentecostal Church which has sixty thousand members, and a choir five thousand strong.

'They are only allowed to come to the main church once a month, taking it in turns, north, south, east and west of the city.' Don explains. 'When we asked the pastor what the Christians did the rest of the month he replied seriously, "They gather in very small meetings in different parts of the city, from six hundred to three thousand in size"!'

The secret of the phenomenal growth from the human standpoint seems to be that every convert is trained to win others. Before the Sunday services they go out on to the street corners and preach, and then take their congregations back to the main meetings, singing as they go. Thus every service has unconverted people in it.

The night Don and Mike ministered, over ten thousand thronged the church. Many responded for salvation and about three thousand sought healing, and were ministered to through a mass prayer.

Leaving Santiago, Alf and his guests took an overnight train to Tcmuco in the southerly regions of Chile.

They arrived in the afternoon, and next morning were given a civic reception in the office of the Regional Director (or Mayor) of Temuco. This man, who was also a military colonel, promised any help they might request while there.

In Temuco meetings had been arranged in various churches, but much of the ministry centred around the indigenous Mapuche Indians, and took place in the open air.

Here Mike's teaching on faith and provision was especially appreciated, as many of the Indians are very poor. Don's message on 'God—the Source of Supply', also spoke directly to the pastors, who at that time faced a serious crisis in the nature of a huge diocesan debt.

Among many who received healing, probably the most amazing were those who came with bad teeth, and afterwards testified that God had filled the teeth. This unusual type of miracle has been reported from time to time in other countries as far removed as England and Australia. But concerning Chile, Don says, 'Dentists are expensive and few and far between. Whenever you pray for the sick, there are always quite a number coming with decayed teeth. The poor and middle class people usually seek out a pastor for prayer rather than attempting to find a dentist. There are hundreds of people in Chile who have had their teeth healed by God. We had lots of people to minister to in this way. . . . I personally wanted to see what sort of filling God put in a tooth, so one young lady offered to show me. . . . I must say I was filled with awe as I looked at this filling which was a glittering shiny silver colour, and had a pattern on the end of it. . . . The filling was very beautifully done and I am sure beyond any human dentist.'

A five-day crusade in a good-sized auditorium crowned the Temuco ministry. After the first day Mike went further south to Valdivia, where he had excellent meetings, one important fruit being the conversion of the president of the University Students' Union.

Meanwhile, Don continued the crusade in Temuco alone. During the five days many sought the Lord and many spectacular healings took place.

Outstanding among these was the healing of a middle-aged man, a polio victim, who had one leg shorter than the other. 'This was not a case of a spine or back needing adjustment to lengthen the leg,' Don emphasizes, 'but three centimetres of leg that weren't there.'

Don sat the man down and held one leg in each hand, closely watched by Dr Bill Maxwell, a Christian doctor. Then, before their eyes, the short leg grew out to match the other.

'Give him a thorough examination before we say any-

174

thing to the crowd,' Don instructed, turning to his doctor friend.

Dr Maxwell, who believes in miracles, examined the man to his own satisfaction, then called another more sceptical doctor acquaintance out from the congregation and invited him to check his findings.

While the two doctors examined the man, Don continued to pray for the sick, watching the amusing spectacle out of the corner of his eye.

They made the man take off his shoes. They pummelled his hips. They stood him up. They sat him down—repeating the performance a number of times. Eventually both doctors, together with the man who had been healed, came to the platform and announced to the congregation that God had certainly worked a miracle. Both legs were now the same length!

The last night, a Sunday, brought the crusade to an exciting climax when one hundred people received the baptism in the Holy Spirit. These included several missionaries and pastors and some of their wives.

As Don moved over to the diocesan bishop, who had also come forward for prayer, he joked, 'It usually takes an archbishop to lay hands on a bishop, doesn't it?'

'Get on with it. I want to be filled,' the other responded, and within seconds, he too was worshipping the Lord in an unknown tongue.

After the great meeting had finally ended, Don and Alf, together with Mike, who had rejoined them for the last day, hurried off to catch a midnight train. Twenty or more believers accompanied them to the station, continuing to sing and praise the Lord as they stood on the platform.

At last the three men managed to say their good-byes and escape inside to their sleeping compartments. Seconds later they heard a commotion outside and realized they were being called out again. They made their way back to the door, and leaned out. There on the platform stood the arch-deacon who all week long had held out against the work of the Holy Spirit.

Now he called to them urgently and began to climb up the steps of the carriage: 'I want to be baptised in the Holy Spirit.' Hurriedly, Don laid his hands upon him and prayed and they just managed to get him off the train before it began to pull out. Their last vivid memory of Temuco was the sight of the ecstatic arch-deacon on the platform praising the Lord in tongues as he waved them good-bye.

The final leg of Don and Mike's itinerary took them to Vina and Valparaiso on the coast. On the way to one meeting in the Union Chapel in Valparaiso the Lord spoke to Don saying, 'I want you to be very dignified tonight.'

It turned out that the congregation was made up mainly of the affluent people of the city. That night twenty people responded and received Jesus as their Lord.

The next day a church member received a phone call from one of the converts, which confirmed the reality of the work done in her heart.

'I'm a race-horse owner,' she informed her hearer. 'Now that I'm a Christian will I have to get rid of my race horses?' 'That's between you and the Lord,' the other responded diplomatically.

'Yes. Well, He's already told me to get rid of them. In fact He has told me I must not sell them but give them away,' she replied.

Much of the ministry in Valparaiso was again to church leaders and to missionaries. Here the teaching concentrated on the baptism and gifts of the Holy Spirit.

One outstanding event was the meeting in the National Park held in a clearing in the woods, with a stream and waterfall close by. Being a bank holiday several Anglican Churches had come together for the whole day. As Don preached and encouraged them on the subject of faith many responded by joining him in praying for the sick. As the people laid hands on one another many were instantaneously healed.

A television interview on a news programme in Valparaiso gave wide publicity to the final four-day crusade, and again the Lord moved mightily by His Spirit in a variety of ways. And then the tour was over.

Don and Mike returned to Santiago, and made their way to the airport where Alf and his wife regretfully said their farewells.

Looking forward to a return visit in the will of God at some later date, Don and Mike headed home for England, feeling 'really fulfilled' and praising Chile as 'the freest country we have ever visited'.

25

It's the Greatest Day You Ever Lived

If you should chance to meet Don Double some morning bright and early, he will possibly hail you with his favourite greeting, 'It's the greatest day you ever lived.'

This saying, not intended to be taken as a joke, is virtually a confession of faith and expresses a deep conviction. Don says, 'Yesterday has gone. Tomorrow is not yet here. We only have today, and today is a great day because it is the day the Lord has made for us to rejoice, and to be glad in.'

The Good News Crusade, nurtured in this optimistic faith, has grown out of all proportion to Don's original intentions. Aiming to keep the team on a small and intimate basis, they decided several years ago to 'grow no more'. 'But,' says Don, 'the Lord's answer to that was that the work mushroomed overnight. . . . It's all too big for me and what I desired. But we are just trying to move along with God and if we move with Him, everything will be fine.'

To keep up with the increasing demand for the ministry of the Good News Crusade team, each department needed extra help, so that by the end of 1979 the whole team—comprising crusade team, administrative team, and overseas missionary personnel—had grown to thirty-six full-time workers.

One of these is Tony Barrett, who has joined the team in the capacity of administrator, together with his wife

Sheila who assists in the bookshop at St Austell.

For some time the Good News Crusade had felt the need for someone to co-ordinate the work in a full-time capacity, but they were determined to await the Lord's appointment.

In advertising this need in *Ripened Grain* in January 1977, they urged that anyone interested should write in giving details of their qualifications, but also cautioned them to wait on the Lord together with the team, and be prepared to receive a 'no' answer with good grace if that was how the Lord should lead.

Mike Darwood wrote, 'It is one of the weaknesses of many churches, fellowships and other Christian organizations to accept every enthusiastic offer to help however unsuitable the person volunteering may be for that particular job, the end result being a collection of round pegs in square holes. We believe that within the body of Christ there is a place for everyone, and that as we walk in the Spirit everyone can be in his place.'

Not surprisingly, a virile and talented team has been building up steadily over the years.

Increased work and workers of course have gradually necessitated more and bigger of everything else. Heather was first in recognizing the need for a bigger house.

The Doubles in addition to their own family of seven (prior to the marriages of their two elder children) also housed David Abbott for quite a long period, making eight for three bedrooms. This, plus the need to accommodate over-night visitors from time to time, led Heather into what Don calls her 'prodding ministry'.

Don had long since decided, 'I'll never move. It's too beautiful here. God gave us this place.' So Heather began to prod gently, 'Don't you think we ought to start believing God for a bigger house? Don't you think we ought at least to pray about it?'

179

But Don, who in actual fact only lived there about ten weeks out of every year, would reply stubbornly, 'No. I'm staying here.' However, he eventually took heed. He told Heather one day, 'The Lord has spoken to me, darling. I'm wrong and you are right. We'll start looking for a bigger house.'

They began their search and looked over a couple of places. Then as they viewed their third prospect the Lord gave them the witness, 'This is it.' Every member of the team when they saw the house reacted in the same way, unanimously agreeing that this was the Lord's choice.

After moving house in May 1975 Don wrote in his monthly letter, 'The children especially appreciated it. They are like birds let out of a cage with room to move and not having to step over one another to get to bed. . . .'

When at the dedication of the new house someone prophesied in the Spirit of further expansion, and of the need in due time for a further move, Don smiled wryly and groaned, 'Oh no, Lord. Let us stay here for a little while at least.'

Another need which became urgent the same year concerned the tent. The five-hundred seater now no longer accommodated the crowds that thronged to the summer crusades and camps. To add another section would have made a grotesque-looking long narrow structure. Instead they decided to trust the Lord for a completely new tent.

By the time they received the estimate, in the region of five thousand pounds, they already had in their hands a cheque for that amount, confirming the Lord's go-ahead.

Early in 1976 they placed their order for a circular thousand-seater tent, and used it for the first time at the Cheltenham crusade. The old tent with one section removed now serves as the prayer tent and connects with the main tent by an enclosed passage way.

The Cheltenham crusade began on a Friday, but they reserved the dedication of the tent until Saturday, when many of their prayer-partners could also be present. More than six bus loads of friends came from different parts of the country for the dedication, and together with the locals made up a congregation of over six hundred.

Graham Evans led the service, representing Vic Ramsey who could not be present. Don's old friend of Ipswich days, the Rev. Martin Simmons, prayed 'a very anointed and powerful prayer of dedication asking God to use the tent to meet the needs of the people'. Rosemary Ellison recalls, 'In particular I remember he asked God to heal and unite families. Betty Lou Mills, the well-known Gospel singer, took up the same theme in a song she sang concerning couples who find themselves without love in their marriages. She ministered that God could put the love back if they looked to Him.'

Several couples responded that same evening and received counselling and prayer for this very problem. And the healing of marriages continues to be a constant phenomenon in the Good News Crusade ministry.

During the Cheltenham crusade numbers ranged from between four to six hundred nightly. Then at the Blaithwaite camp that year eleven hundred people jammed the tent beyond comfortable capacity, hinting loudly that the time might soon come when a new central section would have to be added.

The following year after a tremendous crusade season Don wrote, 'The new tent has already become too small. On two occasions during the Watford crusade we had to turn away people who could not get in. We have already ordered another section for next year and it will seat up to fourteen hundred from then on.'

But expansion presents new problems and challenges. As Don wrote in a prayer letter in 1976, 'Our two vehicles have again become too small and it would be illegal to carry all the equipment in them. Therefore we had to go to Blaithwaite without some. We prayerfully considered the new challenge and saw that the only answer was to sell our transit van that carried seventeen hundredweight and buy a three tonner. . . . The Lord has led us to a brand new one with a £1,000 discount. . . .' Believing it would be wrong to let a good offer slip through his fingers, Don ordered the vehicle in faith laying the need before his prayer partners, and in due time took delivery of the new monster.

Now the team are acutely aware of the need of larger headquarters. Commenting on the mislaying of some correspondence, Don wrote, 'Not a very unusual thing to happen these days, with practically every office having to be shared by two, and sometimes three departments. We really *need* those bigger premises.' Several possibilities are now on the horizon and will doubtless be prayed into reality shortly.

But more impressive than tents or vehicles or buildings is the expansion of the actual scope of the GNC's two-pronged ministry of evangelism and renewal.

Fanning out for conferences and conventions, for non-residential weekends of renewal in churches, and for ministry in schools and colleges and private homes, the various members of the team exercise their God-given ministries which He is pleased to own by confirming the Word with signs following.

In addition, the team are continually answering calls from abroad and during one year alone took in USA, Chile, Greece, Japan and Denmark.

Two new outreaches during 1979 included a Married Couples' Weekend and a Mobile Bookshop. With the high divorce rate in Britain and the satanic attack on family life generally, Don and his team give high priority to teaching on this subject. He and Heather get frequent invitations to address large meetings on the theme of family life, and the Marrieds' Weekends promise to become as popular as Teens and Twenties.

The Mobile Bookshop, based at Hereford, is manned by new team member Dennis Hunting and his wife. It is envisaged that it will travel to agricultural shows, and to Christian camps and churches where there is no bookshop within easy reach, and its first outing to a Christian Caravanners' Club Convention was much appreciated.

Yet another outreach is residential weekends for those desiring to minister in music, led by Tony Mettrick, and assisted by George Telfer who has returned to the team from Africa. A Good News Crusade singing group called The Reapers is also now ministering full time, and making its own impact.

Concerning this enterprise Don says, 'Our intention was to produce a group that could really minister in the power of the Holy Spirit, and with a high standard musically. . . .

'They have also been trained to counsel and pray with people. We intend not that they should entertain Christians, but minister to the Lord at all times.'

In April 1977 GNC produced its first record album of worship music, with Tony Mettrick playing the Hammond Organ and the piano. This was followed by another record entitled *Jesus Is My Music* and featuring soloist Robert Newey of The Reapers. Yet another will feature the whole group.

GNC book publications are also on the increase. In addition to a variety of Bible study books, the team also thought it worthwhile to reprint a famous book on revival, *From Death Into Life* by William Haslam M.A. Simon Matthews has also produced a small book on boy and girl relationships. Don's booklet on the gifts of the Spirit, which has been translated into Swedish and Formosan, was followed by *Discipleship*, dealing with the question of what it means to be a true disciple of Jesus Christ. Another booklet, *After the Prayer of Faith*, attempts to answer questions on healing. During 1979 another section on the fruit of the Spirit was added to *Life in a New Dimension*, the booklet on the gifts, and has been published by Whitaker Press.

Amidst all of the activity and excitement, Don maintains that the tent season is always the high-light of the year's activities, 'being the main burden of our calling from the Lord.'

Although the commission to evangelize the villages has never been rescinded, yet the method of attack has changed somewhat. With the increase of private transport, Don's vision is now to hold crusades in the larger towns, and to saturate the area, taking in the surrounding villages in about a twenty-five-mile radius.

Concerning the 1979 crusades which took place in Brighton, Nene Valley, and Shrewsbury, Don reported, 'At least 2,300 people received some imparting of the life of the Lord Jesus through the tent crusades this summer.' Concerning Nene Valley alone he wrote, 'The miracles of healing included seven in one meeting receiving their sense of smell. . . . Many were baptized in the Holy Spirit . . . there were reconciliations in marriages . . . many declared they were on a new honeymoon. There were quite a number of peole suffering from depression whom the Lord wonderfully delivered, besides a large number who were totally unable to give and receive love. But the Lord wonderfully set them free. . . . It was very encouraging to see at least ten people who were converted to Christ through our ministry in the area over fifteen years ago . . . still going on with God. . . . The most wonderful event of all was our first holy communion service in an evangelistic crusade setting . . . over 600 were present and sixteen clergy leaders from various denominations were there to serve the communion.' At this particular service public reconciliations took place among some of the local clergy, which moved the whole congregation.

Don remarks concerning the enthusiastic response to his crusades, 'It's more like African than English style!'

These joyful and exciting reports contrast oddly with the general pessimism that pervades a large section of the Christian public in England. But however real the gloom in some areas, undoubtedly God is doing a new thing in evangelism, and in the ongoing of renewal in the churches.

Don's attitude to his own calling and that of the Good News Crusade can be best summed up in the following words:

'We are determined by His grace never to compromise the message and to stand four-square on the Word of God at all costs. We want to move with all branches of the church that love the Lord Jesus. We want to see them enter more and more into the centre of His will and to be fully renewed, with the divisions disappearing; that we might visibly be seen to be one body in Christ.

'To this end the teaching ministry has a big part to play, and we are seeing the results more and more as we minister in Britain and around the world.

'"It's the greatest day you have ever lived" is still as firm a conviction with me as it has ever been. God made today for a specific purpose and that is the purpose for which I want to live; for I know that in fulfilling God's purposes, today *will be* the greatest day that I have ever lived.

'I believe the Lord will take us on from step to step and from victory to victory. There is an unfathomable sea of God's grace to be shared with a lost and dying world that is crying out for something real.

'I believe that the message God has given us in the Good News Crusade *is real*. It has the answer. And we can meet the heart's cry of the people and see the world change—as we trust in Him.'

Appendix

The Work of an Evangelist

The ministry of the evangelist is one of the gifts of the risen Christ to his body, the church (Ephesians 4:11). It is a sad fact that in some charismatic circles today this ministry is the most neglected of the five ministries mentioned in that verse, yet I believe that it is essential for a healthy church at any time.

The evangelist is a messenger of a very special kind. The news he brings is good news. He is literally 'a messenger of good'. To evangelize is to proclaim glad tidings, and the evangel is the 'good news'—the Gospel. The Greek word is a composite one, consisting of a word meaning 'well' and another meaning 'messenger'. This second word, when it appears alone in the New Testament, is translated 'angel', and it is interesting to note that in Luke 2:10 an angel proclaims 'good tidings of great joy' to the shepherds. One could call that angel an evangelist! However, a study of Ephesians 4:11 and 12 shows us that the evangelist today has a two-fold ministry: to the church and to the heathen.

A study of the evangelistic ministry of Philip, as recorded in Acts 8:5-40, is very revealing. Some main points are listed below with verse references. I suggest they would make a good basis for a profitable personal or group Bible study.

1. Philip preached 'Christ', not 'about Christ' (verse 5). There is all the difference in the world be-

tween the two approaches; one is life, and other lifeless history.

2. On this occasion the evangelist was preaching to the unconverted—to the heathen (verse 5).

3. When he preached, he gripped the attention of his hearers—there was life in his words (verse 6 and see also Romans 1:16).

4. His preaching was accompanied by miraculous signs (verses 6 and 13; see also Mark 16:19-20).

5. He had authority over evil spirits (verse 7).

6. His preaching brought great joy to those who heard it (verse 8; see also John 15:11).

7. His ministry exposed the occult practices that had been deceiving the people (verses 9-13).

8. Philip did not preach 'easy believism' such as 'come to Jesus and have your sins forgiven'; he preached 'the things concerning the kingdom of God' (verse 12). I believe that a vital part of renewal is always preaching on the kingdom of God, aimed not as just producing 'converts' but citizens of the kingdom.

9. He also preached concerning the name of the Lord Jesus Christ (verse 12; see also Acts 4:10-12).

10. Those who responded positively to his preaching were baptized (verse 12).

11. He did not have an independent spirit, but recognized the boundaries of his own ministry and the need to submit to other ministries. He willingly submitted to Peter and John when they came from Jerusalem, and let them take over the work (verse 14-17). This is a good illustration of the fact that even the most anointed ministries need the other ministries in the body of Christ.

12. He was very sensitive to God's leading (verses 26-29).

13. He was equally concerned to bring the Gospel to a whole city and to one individual (verses 29-30).

14. Whatever scripture came to hand, he preached

Christ from it, that is, a revelation of Jesus (verse 35).

15. He demanded reality from those who responded to his message, and a full commitment to the Lord Jesus Christ (verse 37b).

16. He was an itinerant minister (verse 40).

17. He was a family man who had his family in good order (Acts 21:8-9). His four daughters were morally correct (they were virgins) and they were moving in the things of the Spirit (they prophesied).

18. He was given to hospitality (Acts 21:8-15). He willingly took in Paul and his company for 'many days' and there appears to have been much coming and going, such as the visit of Agabus the prophet. It seems likely that a great deal of ministry went on in Philip's home during Paul's visit!

Luke had no doubt what Philip's ministry was: in Acts 21:8 he calls him 'Philip the evangelist', and I have no doubt that this ministry was recognized both by Philip's local church and by the wider body of Christ. A study of Acts 8:5-40 also convinces me that Philip was himself quite confident of his call, and this is essential for every evangelist. I once met a minister whose preaching was quite lifeless and ineffective. After the meeting I had an opportunity of talking to him. I was very burdened to help him, and I asked him to tell me about his call. He replied, 'Oh, I have not had one of those.' This was a sufficient explanation for the ineffectiveness of his ministry. When God ordains a minister, he calls him, and calls him specifically.

I believe it is of equal significance that Philip's ministry was recognized by others. When God gives a man a ministry, others see it and submit to it. It is also vital that as with every other ministry, an evangelist should be 'sent'. Read Acts 13:1-4 for an account of how Paul was 'sent' on his first missionary journey; and also Romans 10:15—'And how shall they preach except they be sent?'

In this outreach ministry, the evangelist will usually go to places where there is little or no flow of God's life. When he arrives, he will enquire who is worthy (Matthew 10:11) and he will work in conjunction with the local body of Christ, even if that body is but feebly expressed in the area. In many cases today, an evangelist's visit to an area springs from an invitation from members of the body of Christ in that area. If an evangelist is invited by the local body of Christ to visit an area where there is already a real flow of the life of God, then one important aspect of his ministry will be a faith-building ministry to the church (Ephesians 4:12). He will also be concerned that the local church maintains a healthy attitude towards the lost souls in their area, and has a vision for evangelism.

I believe very strongly that when an evangelist visits an area, the spirit of evangelism comes on all the body of Christ in that locality, and that every Christian is anointed to join in the work of evangelism.

Remember, it is sheep that produce lambs, not the shepherd! The believers are the sheep, and the evangelist plays the part of midwife. When God gave me a tent, he told me it was to be a spiritual maternity ward.

I see that the evangelist has a very definite part to play in the present-day spiritual renewal. Jesus said 'I am come that they might have life, and that they might have it more abundantly' (John 10:10). The evangelist should be an able minister of the New Testament 'not of the letter, but of the Spirit: for the letter killeth, but the Spirit giveth life' (2 Corinthians 3:6). In so much evangelism today the letter is accurately presented, but it is the dead letter that kills, and the result is still-born converts. It is not the job of the evangelist to pressurize people through a system, like pushing sausage meat into a machine to turn out sausages. Such an evangelism, which is based on 'believism', does not produce life, which only comes through a thorough repentance and a work of the Holy Spirit.

The evangelist should not be a 'loner', doing his 'own thing'. Philip was one of the seven (Acts 6:5), a member of the local body of Christ. He was quick to call in Peter and John when he saw that their ministry was needed (Acts 8:14-15). The prophet Agabus was welcome at his house, as were Paul and his party (Acts 21:8). It does seem that Philip went to Samaria alone, but I believe that this was only because of the persecution that was going on (Acts 8:4-5). Luke 10:1 makes it clear that the norm is for God's ministers to go at least in pairs. In my own ministry the Lord has given me a team. I did not plan it—He did it—and during our campaigns we have a wonderful experience of body ministry. Our vision is to reach every soul in an area and lead them to a saving knowledge of Christ. That is what Philip experienced (Acts 8:5-6), and I believe that before the return of Christ we shall see it happen again. The nearest I have personally approached to this goal was at a place called Nacasol, in Kenya, where I was told that after my visit there were only four people left unsaved!

The evangelist is a preacher, and 1 Corinthians 1:21 tells us 'it pleased God by the foolishness of preaching to save them that believe'. Paul elaborates on this theme in Romans 10. Verse 14 asks: 'How then shall they call on him in whom they have not believed? And how shall they believe in him of whom they have not heard? And how shall they hear without a preacher?' Verse 17 adds, 'So then faith cometh by hearing, and hearing by the word of God.' It is true that God uses other methods besides preaching to save the lost, but I believe that they are secondary to preaching. The ministry of the evangelist is a manifestation of the wisdom of God: 'He that winneth souls is wise' (Proverbs 11:30). However, while

I am sure that today God is restoring and emphasizing the ministry of the evangelist, it is also true that as Paul told Timothy, we can all do the work of an evangelist (2 Timothy 4:5). Timothy was certainly not an evangelist, but there came a time when he had to be available to the Lord to do the work of an evangelist, and I believe the same is true of each of us.